The Imposture by James Shirley

A TRAGI-COMEDIE.   As it was Acted at the private House in Black Fryers.

James Shirley was born in London in September 1596.

His education was through a collection of England's finest establishments: Merchant Taylors' School, London, St John's College, Oxford, and St Catharine's College, Cambridge, where he took his B.A. degree in approximately 1618.

He first published in 1618, a poem entitled Echo, or the Unfortunate Lovers.

As with many artists of this period full details of his life and career are not recorded. Sources say that after graduating he became "a minister of God's word in or near St Albans." A conversion to the Catholic faith enabled him to become master of St Albans School from 1623–25.

He wrote his first play, Love Tricks, or the School of Complement, which was licensed on February 10th, 1625. From the given date it would seem he wrote this whilst at St Albans but, after its production, he moved to London and to live in Gray's Inn.

For the next two decades, he would write prolifically and with great quality, across a spectrum of thirty plays; through tragedies and comedies to tragicomedies as well as several books of poetry. Unfortunately, his talents were left to wither when Parliament passed the Puritan edict in 1642, forbidding all stage plays and closing the theatres.

Most of his early plays were performed by Queen Henrietta's Men, the acting company for which Shirley was engaged as house dramatist.

Shirley's sympathies lay with the King in battles with Parliament and he received marks of special favor from the Queen.

He made a bitter attack on William Prynne, who had attacked the stage in Histriomastix, and, when in 1634 a special masque was presented at Whitehall by the gentlemen of the Inns of Court as a practical reply to Prynne, Shirley wrote the text—The Triumph of Peace.

Shirley spent the years 1636 to 1640 in Ireland, under the patronage of the Earl of Kildare. Several of his plays were produced by his friend John Ogilby in Dublin in the first ever constructed Irish theatre; The Werburgh Street Theatre. During his years in Dublin he wrote The Doubtful Heir, The Royal Master, The Constant Maid, and St. Patrick for Ireland.

In his absence from London, Queen Henrietta's Men sold off a dozen of his plays to the stationers, who naturally, enough published them. When Shirley returned to London in 1640, he finished with the Queen Henrietta's company and his final plays in London were acted by the King's Men.

On the outbreak of the English Civil War Shirley served with the Earl of Newcastle. However when the King's fortunes began to decline he returned to London. There his friend Thomas Stanley gave him help and thereafter Shirley supported himself in the main by teaching and publishing some educational works under the Commonwealth. In addition to these he published during the period of dramatic eclipse four small volumes of poems and plays, in 1646, 1653, 1655, and 1659.

It is said that he was "a drudge" for John Ogilby in his translations of Homer's Iliad and the Odyssey, and survived into the reign of Charles II, but, though some of his comedies were revived, his days as a playwright were over.

His death, at age seventy, along with that of his wife, in 1666, is described as one of fright and exposure due to the Great Fire of London which had raged through parts of London from September 2nd to the 5th.

He was buried at St Giles in the Fields, in London, on October 29th, 1666.

Index of Contents

TO SIR ROBERT BOLLES Baronet.

Sir,

It hath been a Complement with some, when they have treated Friends, to profess a barrenness in that which they had prepared not without studied charge, and Curio sitie. As I was never so insolent to magnifie my own, being best acquainted with my weak abilities: so I should deserve a just affront to my self, and undervalue your person, to present you with any thing were first cheap in my own opinion. Sir, this Poem, I may with modesty affirm, had a fair reception, when it was personated on the stage, and may march in the first rank of my own compositions, which directed now by my humble devotion, comes from the press to kiss your hand, and bear your noble Name in the dedication. I cannot have so much prejudice upon your nature, to think you will decline it, and should I abate those other characters of honour that shine upon you, your indulgence to Musick and singular love to the worthy professors eminently, shew the harmony of your soul, and while Poetry is received a Musicall part of humane knowledge, I cannot despair of your candid entertainment. Sr. I beseech you take it, as an earnest of my thoughts to serve you, I am assured it brings with it, beside the acknowlegment of your late obligation upon me, ambitious desires to preserve my interest in your favour, while I subseribe my self,

Sir,
The humblest of your Honourers,
James Shirley.

DRAMATIS PERSONAE
Duke of Mantua
Honorio, his Son
Flaviano, The Dukes Creature
Leonato, The Duke of Ferrara's Son
Petronio, a noble man of Ferrara
Bertoldi, an insolent Coward, son to Florelia
Claudio, a creature of Flaviano
Volterino
Hortensio
Colonells
Antonio, a Gentman
Friar
Pandolfo, a servant of the Tavern
Soldiers
Servants

Fioretta, Daughter to the Duke of Mantua
Donabella, Sister to Leonato
Juliana, A Mistris of Flaviavo
Florelia, A noble Lady, Mother to Bertoldi
Abbesse

Ladies

The First Two Acts in Mantua, the Rest in Ferrara.

THE IMPOSTURE

THE PROLOGUE

Our poet not full confident he says,
When Theaters free vote had crown'd his plays,
Came never with more trembling to the stage,
Since that poetick Schism possest the age.
A Prologue must have more wit than the play,
He knowes not what to write, fears what to say.
He has been stranger long to'th' English scene,
Knowes not the mode, nor how with artfull pen,
To charm your airy soules; beside, he sees
The Muses have forsook their groves, the trees
That fear'd no thunder, and were safely worn
By Phaebus own priests, are now rudely torn
By every scurrile wit that can but say
He made a Prologue to a new—no play.
But let 'em pass; you Gentlemen that sit
Our judges, great Commissioners of wit,
Be pleas'd I may one humble motion make,
'Tis that you would resolve for th' authors sake,
I'th' progress of his play not to be such
Who'l understand too little, or too much
But choose your way to ludge; to th' Ladies one
Address from the Author, and the Prologue's done,
In all his Poems, you have been his care,
Nor shall you need to wrinckle now that fair
Smooth Alablaster of your brow, no fright
Shall strike chast eares, or dye the harmlese white
Of any cheek with blushes, by this pen
No Innocence shall bleed in any scene,
If then your thoughts secur'd you smile, the wise
Will learn to like by looking on your eyes.

Mantua – An Apartment in the Palace.

Enter **DUKE**, **HONORIO**, **FLAVIANO** at several Doors.

DUKE
No Army yet discover'd?

FLAVIANO
None.

DUKE
We are lost.

HONORIO
Despair not sir.

DUKE
Away, thy confidence is folly,
Is not danger round about us,
From every part destruction staring us
I'th' face? this City, like a fatall Center,
Wherein the bloody lines of War, and Famine,
Prepare to meet?

FLAVIANO
And every minute we expect a Battery.

HONORIO
The walls are not so easily made dust,
As the besiegers would perswade our faith;
Disarm not your own hearts, my confidence
Tells me we sha' not suffer, the Duke of
Ferrara may send yet to raise the siege.

DUKE
Fond Boy, it was thy counsell to depend
Upon his aids, and promise Fioretta,
Thy Sister, with so great a dowry to
The Dukes vainglorious Son; fame has beli'd
His valour, and we now are cheated of
Our lives and Dukedome.

HONORIO
Sir, with my duty safe, let me intreat you

Not stain the character of a Prince so much;
The interest we have in that great Title
Should make us wise in our belief; for when
Princes break faith, Religion must dissolve,
And nature grone with burthen of the living
Beside his Son Leonato, how ever
Traduc'd or sullied by some Traitors envy,
Deserves a noble fame, and loves the hope
Of our alliance; I ne'r saw his person
But, twere a sin, honor could not forgive
In us to question him.

DUKE
We fool our selves;
Lets think of timely Articles and yield.

FLAVIANO
Whilst there is hope of mercy.

HONORIO
Oh! this want
Of man will make all our well meaning starres
Forfiet their kind aspects, & turn their influence to death

FLAVIANO
My Lord, I cannot be concern'd in name
And honour with your person, whose least blood
Is worth ten thousand arteries of mine,
Therefore while such necessities invade us
I cannot but prefer your lives, and in
My duty counsell, you would think of what
Is offer'd here, rather than hazard all
By a vain expectation of an Army
From Leonato, who with all his forces
Is not yet sure to prosper in our cause.

DUKE
Consider that Honorio.

FLAVIANO
Nay, should Heaven
So smile upon us, that his sword o'r come,
This to weak apprehension may promise
Our glory, but examine well the close,
There may be greater danger in his victory,
Than all our want of him can threaten.

HONORIO

You perplex my understanding.

FLAVIANO
He expects your Sister the reward of his great service.

HONORIO
Is it not Justice?

FLAVIANO
Yes, forbid it goodness,
He should not thrive in his fair hope, and promises;
But if her Highness find not in her heart
Consent, to meet the Prince with love and marriage,
Who shall defend us from his power? that must
Keep us in awe, and this earth, panting yet
With frights and sufferings of the Warre.

HONORIO
It is my wonder Lord Flaviano, your wisdome
Should weave these wild impossibilities;
My Sister not consent? nature, her birth,
Obedience, honor, common gratitude,
Beside ambition of what can be hop'd for
To make her happy, will give wings to her desires.

DUKE
I cannot tell.

HONORIO
I cannot think,
Your reason sir can be so much corrupted,
To look upon my Sister with that fear,
She should not fly to meet our great preserver;
Do you believe, she now 'mong holy Virgins,
Lead thither by her own devotion,
During this Warr to pray, and weep for us
(Teares, whose clear Innocence might tempt an Angel
To gather up the drops, and string for Saints
A Christall Rosarie) can wish us safe
By his victorious arm, without a will
To be her self his own reward? her virtue
Must needs instruct her that, and we apply
No motive to her heart—

[A shout within.

DUKE
What news?

[Enter **CLAUDIO**.

CLAUDIO
From the Watch-tower we descry an Army
Marching this way; the Sun which hath thus long
Muffled his face in clouds, as it delighted
In their approach, doth gild their way, and shine
Upon their burgonets to dazle the faint eyes
Of our beseigers.

HONORIO
'Tis Leonato.

CLAUDIO
Our Enemies, whose Troops circle the Town,
Are making hast to meet 'em, and the Foot
Quitting their trenches, now are gathering
Into a body, as it seemes resolv'd
To give 'em battle.

DUKE
We have life again.
Honorio, collect what strength we have,
And make a sally at your best advantage.
'Tis good to engage 'em both waies.

HONORIO
How my thoughts triumph allready!

[Exit.

DUKE
Now my Son is gone,
Who is not of our Counsell; wee must think
How to behave us, if the Prince succeed,
Our daughter which wee promis'd him in marriage,
Being already sent away, the price
Of his great Victory.

FLAVIANO
Trouble not your self,
Great Sir, your wisdom that inclin'd your faith
To my true Character of the Prince,
And took my counsell for her absence, shall
Applaud my future policy; hee's not come
To conquest yet, however Princes are not
Oblig'd to keep, what their necessities

Contract, but prudently secure their states
And dear posterity; trust to my care,
Fioretta is no match for Ferraras Son,
A Prince deep read in lusts, faithless, and cruell,
So will a Turtle with a Vulture shew,
Or Lamb yoak'd with a Tiger: shee's a pledge
Destin'd by better fate to Crown your age
And heart with blessings Sir.

DUKE
Hark,
The drums talk lowder, from the battlements,
I may behold their fight, and see which Army,
Conquest, now hovering in the air, will mark
Her glorious perch, upon whose Plumed heads
She may advance, and clap her brazen wings.

[Exit.

[Alarum at a distance.

FLAVIANO
Sir I'l attend: Claudio.

CLAUDIO
My Lord.

FLAVIANO
Thou left'st the Princes Fioretta safe at Placentia?

CLAUDIO
Yes Sir.

FLAVIANO
How did she like her progress? thou didst urge
It was my care of her, to take her from
The fright and noise of War.

CLAUDIO
I did my Lord.

FLAVIANO
And did she taste it well?

CLAUDIO
To my apprehension exceeding well,
And gave me strickt commands
To say she will remember, and reward

Your love and care of her.

FLAVIANO
Did she name love?

CLAUDIO
The very word she us'd, and I return'd,
How much your study and ambition was
To merit her fair thoughts.

FLAVIANO
And didst thou scatter, as I instructed
Here and there dark language, to
Dissafect her with the Prince, to whom
The Duke hath rashly made a promise?

CLAUDIO
All; I had fail'd my duty else my Lord.

FLAVIANO
Call me thy friend, thou hast deserv'd me, now
Attend the Duke—so, now my next art must be,

[Exit **CLAUDIO.**

How to come off with with Leonato, if his
Army prevail, the Duke must be instructed;
Honorio thinks his Sister still i'th' Nunnery;
That thought must be preserv'd; a thousand wheels
Move in my spacious brain, whose motions are
Directed by my ambition to possess
And call Fioretta mine, while shallow Princes
I make my State decoyes, then laugh at 'em.

[Alarum, Enter **HONORIO** lead by **CLAUDIO** over the Stage wounded.

The Prince Honorio wounded; fate I bless thee.
How is it with your highness?

HONORIO
I am shot sir.

FLAVIANO
Would it were dangerous—be carefull of him;

[Exit **CLAUDIO** and **HONORIO.**

A curse upon that hand that mist his heart.

HONORIO

So, so, fortune thou shalt have eyes agen
If thou wouldst smile on mischief, I will build thee
An Altar, and upon it sacrifise
Folly and all her children, from whose blood
A curled smoak shall rise, thick as the mists
That breath from Incense to perfume and hide
The sacrifising Priest; sight on,
Ye are brave Fellows, he that conquers may
Get Honor, and deep wounds, but I the day.

[Exit.

SCENE II

The Same. Before the Gates of the City.

[Alarum and Retreat.

[Then Enter **LEONATA, VOLTERINO, HORTENSIO,** and **SOULDIERS** in Triumph, at one door; at the other, enter **MEN** with boughes of Laurell singing before the **DUKE, FLAVIANO, CLAUDIO.**

You Virgins, that did late despair
To keep your Wealth from cruell men,
Ty up in silk your careless hair,
Soft peace is come agen.

Now lovers eyes may gently shoot
A flame that wo'not kill:
The Drum was angry, but the Lute
Shall whisper what you will.

Sing Iö, Iö, for his sake,
Who hath restor'd your drooping heads,
With choice of sweetest flowers make
A garden where he treads;

Whilst, we whole groves of Laurell bring,
A petty triumph to his brow,
Who is the Master of our Spring,
And all the bloom we ow.

DUKE

Our hearts were open sir before the gates
To Entertain you, I see Laurells grow

About your temples, where, as in a grove
Fair Victory Enamour'd on your brow
Delights to sit, and cool her reeking head
And crimson tresses in your shade.

FLAVIANO
The City
In glory of this day shall build a Statue
To you their great preserver, whose tough brass
Too hard for the devouring teeth of age
Shall eat up Time, to keep your fame Eternall;
Our active youth in honor of your name
Shall bring agen the old Olympick games,
And willing to forget what's past in time,
And story, count their years from this dayes triumph,
As if the World began but now; the wives
As if there were no legends past of love,
Shall only talk of you, and your great Valour;
And careless how mans race should be continu'd
Grow old in wonder of your deeds; our Virgins
Leaving the naturall tremblings that attend
On timorous maides, struck pale at sight of blood,
Shall take delight to tell what wounds you gave,
Making the horror sweet to hear them sing it;
Their hands at the same time composing Garlands
Of Roses, Mirtle, and the conquering Bay,
To adorn our Temples, and the Priests, and while
The Spring contributes to their art, make in
Each garden a remonstrance of this battle,
Where flowers shall seem to Fight, and every plant
Cut into Forms of green Artillery,
And instruments of War, shall keep alive
The memory of this day, and your great Victory.
Yet all that can be studied short of you,
Our best, a rude Imperfect Monument
Of your deserved honors.

LEONATO
Y'are too bountifull
In language sir, the service wee have done
May merit your acknowledgment, which though
The Justice of your cause directed first
To this success, was not without a hope
Of a reward you promis'd, and I value it
More than you can esteem all your preservings;
So much hath fame prefer'd your Daughters Virtue
To every excellence.

DUKE
This adds to what
Wee held before excess of honor to us.
I had but a part i'th' Universall benefit
Your Valour gave, but this affection
Falls like a happy Influence on my self
And blood, whose aged streams you fill with blessings.
My Daughter shall be yours, in which I sum
My lives chief satisfaction. My Lord
Go to the house of Benedictine Nuns,
Among whose sweet society our Daughter,
During this War and tumult, went to offer
Her prayers for our deliverance.
I am in a storm, and now must stand (aside)
My desperate fate.

[Exit **FLAVIANO**.

HORTENSIO
I hope shee's not turn'd Nun?

LEONATO
I should not like it.

VOLTERINO
May not we visit the holy house? 'tis pitty so much
Sweet flesh, should be engros'd and barrell'd up
With penitentiall pickle 'fore their time,
That would keep fresh and fair, and make just work
For their Confessions. I do not like the women
Should be cabled up.

HORTENSIO
I think so.

VOLTERINO
I would this Virgin would be peevish now.

HORTENSIO
Why so?

VOLTERINO
That we might ha' some sport among the Leverets.
For I would so inflame the Generall
He were affronted, that wee should have all
Commission to work into the Warren.

LEONATO

We do want a person here, whose name is great
I'th' Register of honor, it would much
Enlarge our present happiness to Embrace him,
Your Son the prince Honorio.

DUKE
'Twas his chance
Upon a sally, when your colours gave
Us Invitation to the Field, and spirited
Our souldiers, to receive a shot, whose cure
May excuse the want of his attendance sir,
Nor will I doubt his wounds are doubled by
The thought he cannot wait upon your person.

LEONATO
He should have honor'd us, and made me proud
To know, whom so much fair desert hath made
Dear in the voice and love of men: but I
Shall not despair to see him. We want
A limb of our own Army, where is Signior
Bertoldi, that came with us to see Fashions?
I hope we have not lost him.

HORTENSIO
Sir, I know not, I fear hee's slain.

VOLTERINO
He wo'not dy so nobly;
He'l nere give up the ghost without a Fetherbed.
He was sick last night at the report we were
But three leagues off the Enemy, and call'd
For a hot caudle I that knew his cold
Disease persuaded him to drink, which he
Did fiercely as I could wish, in hope to see him
Valiant and walk the round, but quite against
Nature his ague shook him more, and all the Drink
Which was the full proportion of a gallon
Came out at's forehead in faint sweat; he had
Not mov'd ten paces, but he fell down backward
And swore he was shot with a cold bullet; how
They rould him like a Barrel back to his Tent,
For levers could not raise him to make use
Of's feet agen, I know not, nor since saw him.

HORTENSIO
I hope hee's still asleep.

VOLTERINO

But when he wakes,
And finds the Army marcht away, He dares not,
Go home agen alone, & how hee'l venture
O'r the dead bodies hither—he has don't.

[Enter **BERTOLDI** with muskets, pikes &c.

BERTOLDI
Where is the General?

LEONATO
Here comes our mirth.

HORTENSIO
A walking Armorie; noble Signior Bertoldi.

BERTOLDI
If you want Pikes or Muskets there, I could
Ha brought field peeces, but I durst not venture
My chine.

LEONATO
Where had you these?

BERTOLDI
Ask, ask the men I kill'd, if they deny
A syllable I'l forswear the Warrs.

VOLTERINO
He has disarm'd and rob'd the dead.

HORTENSIO
A coward has impudence to rob a Church.

VOLTERINO
He durst not take 'em from a man that had
But so much life in him to gasp or grone,
That noise would fright him.

HORTENSIO
I rejoyce Signior, y'are safe come home.

BERTOLDI
I would I were at home, and you get me
Among your Guns agen—how ist Volterino?

[Enter **FLAVIANO**.

VOLTERINO
This news wil much exalt your Mothers heart.

LEONATO
He is return'd but with a melancholy face.
Where is the Princess?

DUKE
Where is our Daughter?

FLAVIANO
Where her devotion I fear will make
This Dukedome most unhappy, if your virtue
Exceed not what is read in other Princes,
It was my fear that place, and conversation,
Would mortisie too much that active heat
Should wait on the desires of high-born Ladies.

LEONATO
The mystery?

VOLTERINO
Do not you find it? they have nunnified her.

FLAVIANO
Sir, your pardon;
She whom first fear and fright of War perswaded
To joyn her prayer and person with the Virgins
In the religious Cloyster, by what art
Or holy magick won, is now resolv'd—

LEONATO
What, hath she vow'd?

FLAVIANO
Untill a year be finished
By revolution of the dayes great guide,
Not to forsake the Nunnery, but spend
Her hours in thankfull prayers to Heaveu for this
Great victory.

VOLTERINO
So, so, It will come to the battery I talk'd on.

DUKE
It cannot be.

LEONATO

It must not be

VOLTERINO
I am of that opinion my Lord,
It must not be, this is a stratagem.

FLAVIANO
She humbly praies you would interpret this
No breach of filiall piety, nor your
Highness a will to wrong so great a merit
As hath engag'd all fortunes here, and lives
To bleed for you, but weigh in your best charity
That duties are first paid to Heaven, the spring
And preservation of what makes us happy,
And she is confident when you consider—

LEONATO
How much my honor suffers, to imploy
The strength I have to punish this affront.

BERTOLDI
A pox upon't, we shall ha' more fighting now

DUKE
I hope you have no thought of any practice
Here to deserve that language?

VOLTERINO
Y'are abus'd.

LEONATO
If you be her Father sir, I must expect
What did ingage me hither, and without
Delayes, or leave this City in a flame.

BERTOLDI
More Fire-works?

LEONATO
In whose Ashes I will bury this foul ingratitude.

DUKE [aside]
We are ruin'd all.

BERTOLDI
There is not so much danger, to be put
In Rank and File with Pye-meat in an Oven,
If a man were certaine to come out agen

Dow-bak'd.

LEONATO
Yet stay. I have considered,
I may have leave to see this Frozen Lady.

DUKE [aside]
We are more undone.

FLAVIANO
Your person may prevail sir,
And by some better charm, gain her consent,
Or if you please not to ingage your self
Upon the trouble of a hasty visit,
The presence of her Father, and what else
We can prepare to keep your smile upon us,
Shall be inforc'd, to clear how much we aim
At the perfection of your wishes.

BERTOLDI
So, so.

LEONATO
Prosper.

FLAVIANO
I have now courage sir to serve your will,
And am o'th' sudden confident.

LEONATO
It pleases.

DUKE
It is impossible Leonata.

[Exit **LEONATO, LEONATO, BEROLDI, VOLTERINO** and **HORTENSIO.**

FLAVIANO
Promise any thing
In such a strait, and not despair to effect it.
Be private men content with their poor Fathom,
Since Heaveu we limit not, why should not Kings
Next Gods, perform the second mighty things?
Your ear—

[Exeunt.

SCENE I

Mantua. A Convent.

Enter **FLAVIANO** and **ABBESSE** with a Letter.

FLAVIANO
You will obey the Dukes command?

ABBESSE
Good Princes,
Punish, not teach us sacrilege; I'l obey
A thousand sufferings ere such a rape—

FLAVIANO
A rape?

ABBESSE
Of honor, Honesty, Religion;
I am plac'd here to preserve, and not betray
The Innocent; should I instead of prayer,
Chast life, the holyness of vow, of discipline,
With those austerities that keep wild blood
In calm obedience, now begin to teach
Soul-murdering liberty, the breach of all
Was promis'd Heaven.

FLAVIANO
Wy' Madam you mistake,
We ask no Virgin to turn Whore, we onely
Desire you would perswade some pretty Nun,
In this extremity, to take upon her
The Princess Fioretta, whom Leonato
Ne'r saw, and be his Wife in honest marriage.

ABBESSE
Can you be thus
Unjust to him, so late preserv'd your lives?

FLAVIANO
Trouble you not your reverend head with that,
He shall be satisfied, and you remain
Still mother of the Maid, no more sour faces,
But turn your wit to'th' bufiness.

ABBESSE
Never sir.

FLAVIANO
Take heed and have a care of this inclosure,
The Dukes breath makes all flat, tis yet no common;
You are old, and should be wise.

ABBESSE
I would be honest.

FLAVIANO
Shew it in your obedience; will you do't?

ABBESSE
Never.

FLAVIANO
D'ee hear? I sent unto this holy place,
A Damzel call'd Juliana, she's in your Catalogue,
And yet but in probation, cause I see,
You make so nice a conscience, so severe,
I'th' rules of honesty, and would not have,
Your Virgin province touch'd with least defilement,
Pray let me speak with her, it will concern you.

ABBESSE
Would you pervert her?

FLAVIANO
I know not what you call perverting,
But she has not too much Nuns flesh,
And tis my charity to your chast Order
To give you timely notice.

ABBESSE
What do I hear?

FLAVIANO
No more than you may justifie in time,
If things prove right, she was a merry soul
And you ha' not spoild her, if you mean to be
No Midwife, let me talk with her a while.

ABBESSE
Protect us Virgin thoughts

[Exit.

FLAVIANO

So, so, this was reserv'd to wind up all,
It may be fortunate;
I know her spirit high, and apt to catch at
Ambitious hopes and freedom, some good counsell
May form her to my purpose, I have plung'd
Too farre, to hope for safety by return,
I'l trust my destiny to the stream, and reach
The point I see, or leave my self a rock
In the relentless waves; shee's here, I'm arm'd.

[Enter **JULIANA** and **ABBESSE**.

JULIANA

By your own goodness, reverend Mother give
No belief to him; though he be a great man,
He hath not been held guilty of much virtue,
Yet tis my wonder he should stain my Innocence;
Pray in your presence, give me leave to acquit
My Virgin honor; for the wealth of all
The World, I would not have this shame be whisper'd
To the stain of our profession.

[Enter **NUNNE**.

NUNNE

Madam, the Duke

ABBESSE

The Duke?

FLAVIANO

Peace to the fair Juliana.

[Exit **ABBESSE** and **NUNNE**.

JULIANA

Y'are not noble,
A most dishonord Lord, your titles cannot
Bribe my just passion, who will trust a man?
Oh sir, you are as black, nay have a soul
As leprous with ingratitude, as the Angels
Are white with Innocence; was't not enough
To rob me of my honor, the chief wealth
Of Virgins, and confine me to my tears,
Which ne'r can wash away my guilt (should I
Live here to melt my soul into a stream

With penitence) but when I had resign'd
The World with hope to pray, and find out mercy,
You must thus haunt me with new shame and brand
My forehead here, as if you meant to kill
My better essence by despair, as you
Have stain'd my body.

FLAVIANO
Deer Juliana I
Confess I injur'd thee thou knew'st no sin
But from my charm, 'twas only I betraid thee
To loss of thy dear honor, then of liberty,
For 'twas my practice, not thy pure devotion
Made thee a Recluse first; but let not passion
Lose what I would not only save from shipwrack,
But make as happy as thy thoughts can wish thee;
By thy wrong'd self tis true, nor could I choose
Another way than by discovery
Of both our shames to right thee, I am come
To make thee satisfaction in so high
And unexampled way of honor, thou
Shalt say I did deserve to be more wicked,
When thou hast weighed the recompence.

JULIANA
You amaze me

FLAVIANO
Collect thy senses, and discreetly mind me;
Thou canst not be concern'd so much alive
In any other story, hear me gently
And prize the wealth of every syllable.

[Takes her aside.

[Enter **DUKE** and **ABBESSE**.

ABBESSE
Had you been pleas'd to have left your daughter still
My charge and sweet companion, I should
Have left no duty unessay'd, to have shewn
In what degree I honor'd her, but I
Must not dispute your royall pleasure, though
With some sad thoughts to separate, I resign'd her
To your commands.

DUKE
It was your virtue Madam, she found no

Consent to be profest, nor love the Prince,
To whom I promis'd her a Wife, although
Our fears keep warm his hope, in his belief
Shee's here inclos'd still, but without thy help,
We are all lost.

JULIANA
The Prince Leonato?

FLAVIANO
Ther's a preferment, this is considerable.

JULIANA
If you my Lord be serious; a Princess!
The change would do well.

FLAVIANO
Be but confident to manage it.

JULIANA
Hath he not seen the Princess by picture?

FLAVIANO
Never.

JULIANA
Strange!

FLAVIANO
'T was a ceremony, in the necessities of our state,
The Duke ne'r thought on, & I meant not to insert it,
As knowing Fioretta had no zeal,
To what her Father darkly had contracted;
His Highness doth expect thee.

JULIANA
It would be
More for my honor, if he took the pains,
To visit our Religious house, and then—

FLAVIANO
It shall be so.

JULIANA
But twill be necessary,
You purge me to the Abbesse, no suspition,
Must live within her thought.

FLAVIANO
I apprehend;

[Comes forward with **JULIANA**.

Oh! you have shot a trembling through my soul,
I dare not kiss your hand, the Earth you tread on,
Would too much grace the lips have so prophan'd you.
Madam your pardon; sir be you the witness,
I have wrong'd this noble Virgins honor,
It was my anger, and revenge upon
Your goodness that so late oppos'd me made
Me careless, where I flung disgrace and scandall,
Thus I implore her mercy and forgiveness,
Take her white thoughts to your agen, she is
As innocent from sinfull act by me
As the chast womb that gave me life.

DUKE
Tis piety,
Thus to restore the Innocent, I conceive not
His aym in this.

ABBESSE
Tis satisfaction.

JULIANA
When I stray from your sweet precepts—

ABBESSE
In, I am confirm'd.

[Exit **JULIANA**.

FLAVIANO
All to our expectation, shee's prepar'd,
A Mistris for the Prince.

DUKE
But now I think on't
She must not marry him, it will breed ill blood.

FLAVIANO
By all means marry him, there's no other way
To send him hence, and quit us of the Army,
I'l instantly acquaint him how I prosper.

[Exit.

DUKE
It must not be, my honor will bleed for it.
I have been too much guided by Flaviano.
Madam—

ABBESSE
Your face is troubled.

DUKE
No, my heart
Which you may curc with honor, as I have
Contriv'd it now—

ABBESSE
I shall study with my loss of life
To gain your bosom peace.

DUKE
I like this Virgin,
I know my Lord here hath been practising,
But finds her not inclin'd to that extent
We had propos'd, she is virtuous, you shall
Counsell her onely but to take the name
Of my Fioretta, but not change her life
To marry with the Prince; I do believe,
Her chast, Oh let your goodness keep her still so,
And fortifie her vertuous thoughts, I doubt not
But she with holy eloquence, and pretence
Of vow, and Virgin sanctity,
May so prevaile upon him both to save her self,
Our honors, and the Kingdom from a sacrifice.
May not this be?

ABBESSE
Such extremes I know not.

DUKE
If she persist a chast, and noble Virgin,
You must dispence, we have but little time
For pause, unless this present care be found,
We all must bleed to death upon the wound.

[Exeunt.

SCENE II

An Apartment in the Palace

[Enter **BERTOLDI**.

BERTOLDI
Hum! shall I never fight? drink wo'not do't,
No nor a Whore the greater provocation;
I speak it to my shame, I never durst
Fight for my wench, yet Gentlemen commend
My confidence at paying of a reckoning,
There I can kill 'em all with curtesie,
Discharge my Peeces like a Mr. Gunner at a great supper,
Yet I am not valiant, this must be mended someway.

[Enter **VOLTERINO**.

Volterino? a word.
Tis not unknown to you, that I am a coward.

VOLTERINO
No, not a coward, but you, are not sir,
If I were put to answer upon Oath,
So valiant altogether as Don Hercules,
That strangled a great Bull with his forefinger
And's Thumb, and kil'd the King of Troys great Coach horse
With a box o'th' car.

BERTOLDI
Pox on't, do not abuse me, I shall take it
Scurvily and you deny it.

VOLTERINO
But you wo'not beat me.

BERTOLDI
Ther's the thing, I know't
As well as you can tell me, I am base,
And in plain terms a coward.

VOLTERINO
Why dost not beat thy self for being one?

BERTOLDI
Then I durst fight; no, I was begotten
In a great Frost, between two shaking Agues,
I never shall be valiant, who can help it?
But when you come home agen, if you will but

Swear I am valiant—

VOLTERINO
You shall pardon me.

BERTOLDI
Come, my Mother shall make you amends; a ha,
You love her, she's a Lady and a Widdow,
That has the Goldfinches, hark in your ear,
You shall have her.

VOLTERINO
Shall I have her?

BERTOLDI
A word to the wise.

VOLTERINO
Would I were sure on't.
If I have thy Mother, I will not only swear thou art,
But make thee valiant.

BERTOLDI
Would it were possible, upon that condition
You should ha' my Sister too.

VOLTERINO
She's dead.

BERTOLDI
If she were alive I mean—

VOLTERINO
Farewell, wee'l treat agen, and if I live
Thou shalt be Julius Caesar.

[Exit.

[Enter **HORTENSIO**.

BERTOLDI
When I dye, thou shalt be Caesar's heir.
Noble Hortensio.

HORTENSIO
I am in hast, what's the matter?

BERTOLDI

There lies your way, a hundred thousand Ducats
Will find entertainment somewhere else.

HORTENSIO
Canst thou help me to 'em?

BERTOLDI
Yes, and a better business.

HORTENSIO
How? where noble Bertoldi?

BERTOLDI
Wy—but you are in hast.

HORTENSIO
No, no, where is all this money?

BERTOLDI
Safe enough in a place.

HORTENSIO
But how shall I come by it?

BERTOLDI
You know my Mother.

HORTENSIO
The rich Lady Florclia, the Court Widdow,
Shee's my Mistris.

BERTOLDI
You shall have her.

HORTENSIO
Shall I?

[Enter **LEONATA**, **FLAVIANO**, **VOLTERINO**.

BERTOLDI
Yes, and be Master of as much money
As will make you mad.
The Prince, hark in your ear.

[They walk aside.

FLAVIANO
I knew I should prevail, and I am happy,

There's no frost now within her, if your excellence
Would grace the Monastery with a visit
And satisfie your self, your presence will
Perfect the business, and be a just excuse
To some nice ceremonies that detain
Her Person to comply with virgin modesty,
The Duke will meet you there.

LEONATO
I will attend him.

FLAVIANO
You will consider Sir it is a place
Not us'd to publique treaties, though dispenc'd with
For this your solemn view, and conference,
Your person may be trusted there, without
A numerous train.

LEONATO
You shall direct me Sir.
Volterino, you shall only wait upon me.
Sir when you please.

FLAVIANO
I'm proud to be your conduct.

[Exit **LEONATO, FLAVIANO, VOLTERINO**.

BERTOLDI
You shall have her
And her Estate, that's fair, she has enough
To undo the Devill if he go to law with her,
My Father's dead and has told him that already.

HORTENSIO
I'l do't.

BERTOLDI
Here's my hand, my mother's thine.

HORTENSIO
Not my mother.

BERTOLDI
She shall be any thing I'l have her,
Do you but perswade her I am valiant,
And I'l venture to beat her, and she dare
Deny to marry any man I please

To call my Father in law.

HORTENSIO
Let's walk and think on't.

BERTOLDI
You may swear any thing,
And you pawn your soul for me,
You know you cannot be a loser.

[Exit.

SCENE III

The Convent.

[**NUNNES** discovered singing

O fly my soul, what hangs upon
thy drooping wings,
and weighes them down,
With love of gaudy mortall things?
The Sun is now i'th' East, each shade
As he doth rise,
Is shorter made,
That Earth may lesson to our eyes:
Oh be not careless then, and play
untill the Star of peace
Hide all his beames in dark recess;
Poor Pilgrims needs must lose their way,
When all the shadowes do entrease.

[During the song, enter **DUKE**, **LEONATA**, **FLAVIANO**, and **VOLTERINO**. After the Song, enter **JULIANA**, **ABBESSE**, and **NUNNES**.

LEONATO
She is exceeding fair, what pitty 'twere
Such beauty and perfection should be
Confin'd to a melancholy Cell: I approach
You Madam with the reverence of a votary,
You look so like a Saint, yet nature meant
You should not with such early hast translate
Your self to heaven, till earth had been made happy
With living modells from your excellent figure.
You that become a cloud, and this dull dress
So well, whose sight doth pale, and freeze the blood,

How will you shine to admiration
Of every eye, when you put on those Ornaments
That fit your name and birth? if like a statue
Cold and unglorified by art, you call
Our sense to wonder, where shall we find eyes
To stand the brightness, when y'are turn'd a shrine,
Embellisht with the burning light of Diamonds,
And other gifts that dwell like starres about you?

JULIANA
If you do fancie me an object so
Prodigious, for the safety of your eyes
And others, tender-sighted, give consent,
I may not change this poverty and place,
(More pleasing to my self, than all the pride
Can wait those Goddesses, at Court you bow to)

LEONATO
And yet 'twere heresie in me to say
You could receive addition or glory
By the contributary blaze of Wealth,
Or other dress, which art and curiosity
Can form; you are not by them grac'd, but they
By you made beautifull. Iewells near your eye,
Take soul and Lustre, which but once remov'd
Look dull as in their quarry.

FLAVIANO [aside]
He is taken.

LEONATO
I now applaud my fate, and must account
My undertaking in this War to save
Your Dukedom, but the shadow of a service,
When I consider my reward. Oh! hast
To make me Envi'd of the World, and once
Possest of you, to undervalue all
But Heaven, of which you are the fairest copy.

JULIANA
My Lord, our study here is life, not language,
And in that little time I've had of practice,
My tongue hath learn'd simplicity, and truth;
You are a Prince, and in your Creation
But one degree from Angels, strive to rise
That one round higher, and y' are perfect; I am
By my good Fathers leave, and the sweet rules
Of this Religious order, now i'th' way

To meet another Bridegroom, before whom
While you stand a competitor, you fall
To Atomes; sir my love is planted here,
And I have made a vow, which your own charity
Will bid me not to violate, (your triumph
Being the spring of my imperfect duty,)
That for a year, I'l spend my time among
This happy Quire, to offer up my Prayers
And humble gratitude to Heaven, a weak
Oblation for our safeties.

FLAVIANO
Ha! how's this?

LEONATO
My Lord, did you not say you had prevail'd?
What mockery is this?

FLAVIANO
I am undone.
What does the Gipsey mean, shee'l betray all [aside].
Most excellent Madam.

JULIANA
Oh my Lord imploy
Your counsell, to advance not Kill our Virtue,
Remember where, and what I am.

FLAVIANO
So, so.

VOLTERINO
Sir will you suffer this? a new affront.

JULIANA
I am resolv'd
To live and pay you better tribute here
For your affection, and unequal'd service.
Here no distraction will afflict my prayers,
Which trust me I will offer chastly for you,
At every hour of my devotion.
'Tis you, next Heaven, that gave this blessing to us,
To meet, and in the holy Quire breath up
Our sacred Hymes, while Angells Eccho to us,
And Heaven delighted with our harmony,
Opening her azure curtaines will present us
A vision of all the joyes we pray and hope for.

FLAVIANO [aside]
This my instructions?

JULIANA
O think my Lord
To what a loss of Heaven your love invites me,
Yet let me not be thought while I pretend
The choice, and sweetness of a Recluse, I
Should in a thought accuse your worth, who are
The man of all the World I most could fancie;
If I be seen to blush, make it no sin,
I know it is but honourable love
Wings your desire, and that which should prefer you,
Is merit of your Sword that cut our way,
To freedom and soft peace, Religions Pillow,
The Nurse of Science, and the generall blessing,
You have a title yet more strong pleads for you,
The contract, and the promise of a Prince
A chain with many Links of Adamant.

DUKE
I like not that.

JULIANA
To bind and make me yours,
When I have nam'd these severall interests,
And look upon my self so short of merit,
I chide your unkind destiny, at such
Expence of honor to go off unsatisfied,
And quickly should despise my self the cause
Of your distast, but that my vow confirms me,
And mustring up Religious thoughts prevailes,
Above my other will, made to obey you,
Tis but a year my Lord, that I have bound
My self this exile.

LEONATO
Tis an age.

JULIANA
But while Time hath one minute in his Glass of that,
Nothing shall take me hence, unless you bring
An impious strength upon this holy dwelling,
And force me from my cell, but you are far
From such a sacrilege, oh think not on it,
I'l place you in my heart while you are virtuous,
But such an Act might lose those noble thoughts
Of you I wish preserv'd, but I offend,

And am too large in this unwelcome argument,
May wisdom guide your Princely thoughts,
Whilst I return to pray for you.

[Exit with **ABBESSE** and **NUNNE**.

FLAVIANO
She has o'erthrown all.

VOLTERINO
Sir, if you love her she
Hath taught you a cunning way to make her yours,
This habit is compel'd, a little force,
For form will disingage her, she does love you,
And pleaded hansomely against her self.

LEONATO
No more—I'l not despair yet of your Daughter,
This is but Virgin nicety, at the next
Meeting she may incline to smile upon me,
Shee's too much treasure to be won at first
Assault, Volterino.

[Exit **LEONATO, VOLTERINO, HORTENSIO.**

DUKE
Flaviano.

FLAVIANO
I did expect a storm.

DUKE
We are not safe yet.

FLAVIANO
I wonder why Juliana kept not promise,
The Dog-dayes thaw her chastity, I'm mad,
Oh for some stratagem to save all yet,
But you Sir (give me leave to say) are timorous,
Princes should fix in their resolves, your conscience
Should be as subject to your will, as I am.

DUKE
I must confess Flaviano I had
No fancy to Juliana's marriage.

FLAVIANO
That was all my hope, how could I love the man

Durst kill him now!

[Noise within.

DUKE
I shudder, what noise is that?

FLAVIANO
These horrors will eternally affright us.

[Enter **LEONATO, BERTOLDI VOLTERINO, HORTENSIO**, with swords drawn.

LEONATO
The man that dares be guilty of least Insolence,
To any Virgin, dyes.

[Exeunt **LEONATO, VOLTERINO** and **HORTENSIO**.

BERTOLDI
My hopes are nipt, I thought to have tasted,
Nuns flesh, but the General has made it fasting day.

[Exit.

FLAVIANO
I hope he means to force away Juliana—

[Cries within.

Ha! they attempt it, prosper 'em deer fate.
Blest beyond expectation.

DUKE
Dost think,
We shall be safe.

[Enter **LEONATA, JULIANA** in her habit, **VOLTERINO, HORTENSIO**.

LEONATO
Injoy the other benefit of my Sword
In peace, this shall be mine.

[Exit **LEONATO, JULIANA, VOLTERINO, HORTENSIO**

FLAVIANO
The stars dote on us.

[Enter **HONORIO** and **CLAUDIO**.

HONORIO
What unexpected tumults fright the City?

DUKE
You are too bold upon your wound Honorio
To come abroad.

FLAVIANO
The Prince has stoln your Sister
From the Nunnery.

HONORIO
He dares not
Blemish his honor so, though he deserv'd her,
And all our lives, should she be obstinate.

FLAVIANO
Tis done.

HONORIO
This Act shall lose him, death upon
The Surgeon, that hath dallied with my wounds,
But I'l revenge this rape.

[Exit with **CLAUDIO**.

DUKE
Look to the Prince.

[Exit.

FLAVIANO
I could adore my destiny, the wench sure,
Meant to be ravish'd thus, I kiss thy policy;
This chance hath made a dancing in my blood,
While sin thrives, tis too early to be good.

[Exeunt.

ACT III

SCENE I

Ferrara. An Apartment in the Palace.

Enter **ANTONIO** and **FIORETTA**.

FIORETTA
Is this Ferraras Court?

ANTONIO
Yes Madam.

FIORETTA
I will not yet discover, I shall find,
A time Antonio to reward thy faith
And service to me.

[Enter **DONABELLA, FLORELIA, LADIES.**

ANTONIO
Here are Ladies Madam.

DONABELLA
I have a great desire to see this wonder,
The Princess Fioretta, so much fam'd
For beauty.

FLORELIA
Comes she with his Excellence?

DONABELLA
Most certainly, so speaks the Prince Leonato's
My Brothers Letters, and that with some difficulty,
He gaind her from the Nunnery.

FLORELIA
Who is this?

DONABELLA
She has an excellent shape, some stranger;
Prethee Florelia ask.

ANTONIO
This Lady Madam,
Seems to make some address this way;

[Walks aside. **FLORELIA** advances and speaks with **FIORETTA**.

I know not,
Upon what Jealousie my Lady left [aside]
Placentia so privatly, where she
Was entertain'd by Flavianos Mother,

Though old, a Lady of no decrepit brain.

FIORETTA [Whispers him]
Antonio.

FLORELIA
A Lady, Madam, calls her self Lauriana,
Born in Placentia, but the Warrs affrighting,
Both Mantua and the confines, she came hither
With confidence of safety, till the storm
At home be over.

[Exit.

DONABELLA
It is not fit a person of your quality
And presence should be ingag'd to common persons,
And if I may entreat, you shall consent
To be my guest at Court, which will be proud
To entertain such beauty.

FIORETTA
It must be
Too great an honor Madam.

DONABELLA
Leonato my Brother hath secur'd your peace at home,
Which cannot be less pleasing, if you tast
The freedom I can here provide and promise you,
We expect him every minute with the Princess
Fioretta, in whose love he holds more triumph

FIORETTA
And yet his fame was Earlier than this conquest,
For many noble Virtues, but has your grace
A confidence that he brings Fioretta with him?

DONABELLA
Since he left Mantua we received such letters.

[Enter **PETRONIO**.

PETRONIO
Madam, the Prince is come to court, and with him
The gallant Lady wee expected.

FIORETTA
I am not well o'th' suddain.

DONABELLA
Virue defend!

PETRONIO
The good old Duke your Father, will
Shew comfort in his sick-bed to behold
A Son and Daughter.

FIORETTA
Are they married?

PETRONIO
No Madam, but I am confident
So great a joy will not be long deferr'd,
'Twere sin such hope should wither by delay,
They both wish to be happy in your presence,
And you at first sight of this Princely sister
Will much applaud your brothers fate.

DONABELLA
I hope so,
How is it Madam yet?

FIORETTA
I do beseech you
Let not your graces too much care of me
Detain you from the joy your brother brings.
Another Fioretta?

[Enter **LEONATA**.

LEONATO
Donabella?

DONABELLA
I shall not fear a surfet in my joyes
To see you safe.

FIORETTA [aside]
A gallant Gentleman.

LEONATO
What Ladie's that?

DONABELLA
A stranger, sir, with whom I have prevail'd
To grace our court a while, which will be Honor'd

In such a guest.

LEONATO
And I should call it happiness
If you would please to dwell for ever with us,
I have brought home such a companion,
For both your beauties you will not repent.

FIORETTA
The Duke of Mantuas Daughter, I congratulate
Your double victory, and if I may,
Without imputed flattery speak my thoughts,
You did deserve her, had she to her birth,
All the additions that grace a Woman.

LEONATA
You have conferr'd a bounty on me Madam,
And leave me hopeless to reward the debt
I owe this fair opinion.

FIORETTA
Sir, the venture
You made through blood, and danger, doth deserve it,
And she were impious, did not think her self
Much honor'd to be call'd your valors triumph.
I shall betray my self. Censure me not,
Immodest or suspectfull of her virtue,
Whom you have made the darling of your heart.

[Enter **BERTOLDI**.

BERTOLDI
Sir the Duke calls for you.

DONABELLA
Signior Bertoldi.

BERTOLDI
Your Graces creature.

LEONATO
Will it please you Madam?

FIORETTA
I humbly pray your Highness to excuse me,
I may have time and happiness to attend you,
When with more health I may present my services,
I dare not see this Lady.

LEONATO
Wait you upon that Lady Signior.

BERTOLDI
With all my heart; incomparable Lady—
FIORETTA
I have servants to attend me.

BERTOLDI
But not one,
More humble, or more active for your service,
You cannot choose but know my Lady Mother;
I have not seen her yet, but she shall stay,
I'l kneel to her when I have done with you.

[Exit

SCENE II

A Room in Florelia's House.

[Enter **FLORELIA** and **VOLTERINO**.

FLORELIA
But is my Son so valiant, Signior?
This War hath wrought a miracle upon him.

VOLTERINO
He was a coward beyond Ela, Madam,
I must acknowledg, to whom men in pitty
Of his Birth, and care of your much-loved honor
Often forgave his life, but see the turn,
He that went forth (for all our conjurings
And promise of no danger) as he had
Been marching towards Aetna, nay before
The instant fight would have given all the World
To have been assur'd when he came home, but one
Of every thing about him—

FLORELIA
What d'ee mean?

VOLTERINO
One eye, one ear, one arm, and but one leg
To have hopt home withall, strange, how i'th' heat

O'th' Battle he grew double, and there fought
As he had two soules; oh! had you seen
When like a Magazine he march'd, with pikes
With guns & Corslets, which he took from th' Enemy,
With swords more than a Surgeons sign, stuck round,
And seeming like a porcupine to shoot
The Iron Quills—

FLORELIA
But is this possible?

VOLTERINO
I never saw a Dragon do such thing.

FLORELIA
This was not by instinct, but some example
He saw in you, that wak'd his sleeping spirit.
And he must owe all that is Valiant in him
To your brave soul, which like a burning Comet
Flew with prodigious terror to the Enemy.

VOLTERINO
You do not Jeer your servant?

FLORELIA
And so he, by your great blaze
Saw his next way to honor;
Nor can I but acknowledge all my joyes
Now in my Son do flow from you; a souldier
Was ever high in my esteem, but you
Have plac'd the title nearest to me, pray
Favour me often' with your visit.

VOLTERINO [aside]
The Town's my own.

FLORELIA
No complement good Signior, your love
If plac'd on me, shall find an object, though,
Not equall to your favors, not ingratefull;
I wonder he absents himself so long.

VOLTERINO
My care shall be to find him out and bring him
A welcome present to your eye. She's caught.

[Exit

FLORELIA
These Soldiers think if they but once lay siege,
We must come in by force or composition.
Although a Maiden Town may not hold out,
A Widdow but well victualled with the bare
Munition of her tongue, will tire an Army;
I must suspect my Son, for all this legend,
No mighty man at armes; hee's here.

[Enter **BERTOLDI**, **HORTENSIO**.

HORTENSIO
Your blessing.

FLORELIA
Take it, and with it all my prayers, thou maist
Grow up in honor, and deserve to be
Thy Fathers Son.

BERTOLDI
Kiss her Hortensio, do, she is thine own.

HORTENSIO
'Twas my ambition Madam
To wait upon my Convert, and to kiss
Your white hand.

FLORELIA
Signior Volterino was here but now, and has
Told me such stories, Son—

BERTOLDI
Of me?
He had better eat my Spaniard, then mention me
With any scruple of dishonour.

FLORELIA
He extolls you for a Soldier, and tells me wonders.

HORTENSIO
If you dare believe me Madam, your Son has
Behav'd him like a Gentleman.

BERTOLDI
I confess,
I was—but that's no matter, thank this Cavalier;
I can receive and give a gash, and look on't
When I ha' don without your cordial waters

Shall I cut you o'r the face Mother?

FLORELIA
Sir I am poor to recompence the honor
You have done my Son, I see he is your convert,
You that infus'd a soul in him cannot
Enough be glorified.

HORTENSIO
'Tis within your power
Madam to overpoise all my deserts.
True, I did stir those dormant seeds of nobleness
Your blood left in him, and made glow those sparks,
Into a flame, were hid in hills of Ashes;
Now he is yours, and if you Madam think
I have done any service by an Act
Or precept that could light your Son to honor,
You make me fortunate, and encourage
A Souldier to imploy his whole life here.

FIORETTA
How d'ee mean?

HORTENSIO
Without more complement to love you, and—

FLORELIA
What?

HORTENSIO
Wish my self with you Madam when you dream

FLORELIA
You would be with me when I dream.

HORTENSIO
But I should wake you.

FLORELIA
But I should be very angry to have my sleep broke.

HORTENSIO
But I would please you agen,
And rock you into a traunce with so much harmony,
You shall wish to dye in't. I am very plain.

FLORELIA
Me thinks you are very rough.

HORTENSIO
A Souldiers garb,
The old but the best fashion; a Sword,
And flattery were not meant for one mans wearing;
Madam I love you, but not doat upon you,
For you are something old.

FLORELIA
I am indeed sir.

HORTENSIO
Yet you are very handsome, and I love you;
Y'are witty, fair, and honest, but a Widdow,
And yet I love you; I do know you are rich,
Exceeding mighty rich.

FLORELIA
And yet you love me?

HORTENSIO
But Madam, I am a man.

FLORELIA
I do not mean to try you Signior,
Pray Son do you.

HORTENSIO
Now put your vote in.

BERTOLDI
What should I do Madam?

FLORELIA
Try whether he be a man or no.

BERTOLDI
Should I?

FLORELIA
D'ee hear? they say you are grown valiant,
Upon my blessing I command you strike
This Gentleman, and do it presently.

BERTOLDI
Strike him?

FLORELIA

Yes.

BERTOLDI
A way, away, what here?

FLORELIA
Even here, this very minute.

BERTOLDI
Not for your house, and all the monies in't,
Not for my Fathers Wardrob, and I were
An Adamite a top o'th' Alps, though you
Admire the reliques, and have turn'd your Gallery
Into a Chapel, where his severall suites
Hang up like Images for you to pray to:
Strike one taught me to fight!

[Exit **FLORELIA**

HORTENSIO
Is she gone? what said she?

BERTOLDI
The foolish woman—

HORTENSIO
Why what's the matter?

BERTOLDI
Shee shews her breeding, but do not you despair.

[Enter **FLORELIA**.

FLORELIA
If I mistake not sir, you would pretend
You love me honourably.

HORTENSIO
May I perish else.

FLORELIA
When you can make't appear in visible wounds
Upon your head' or body, that my Son
Dares fight—you and I'l be maryed.

BERTOLDI
I told you Signior you should have my Mother.

HORTENSIO
The Devill shall have you both upon easier conditions;
Visible wounds upon my head or body?

FLORELIA
And here's my hand upon the sight thereof,
I'l be your wife; and so farewel till dooms-day.

HORTENSIO
But hark you Lady

BERTOLDI
My Mother's a Witch. I shallne'r be valiant
In this World, what quarrels I may have i'th' next,
I know not,
There are some dead threatned to cudgell me.

HORTENSIO
Is there no hope, that I may catch you in
The Noose of Matrimony, unless your Son
First break my head?

FLORELIA
I wo' not swear.

HORTENSIO
It is not your best course, take heed of vows.

FLORELIA
Why my dear Signior?

HORTENSIO
For your souls sake, and yet
Dispose that as you please, I'l see who dare
Cary your body from me, spight o' Lucifer
I will ha' that, and come by't lawfully;
And so my service; think on't.

[Exit.

FLORELIA
A fine fellow.

[Exit.

BERTOLDI
Would I had his audacity; my Mistris,
Yet knows not what I mean, but I will to her,

And kiss her Glove immediatly.

[Exit.

SCENE III

A Part of the Palace.

[Enter **HONORIO**.

HONORIO
This Court is like a twilight, where I cannot
Distinguish day, or perfect night, some faces
Are cheerfull as the morn, others agen
Are dark, and wrapt like evenings in a mist
· s is instinct for my approach, that brings
A resolution to revenge the rape
Upon my Sister; grow more strong my thoughts,
And let no fear distract you. Prince I have
Consider'd thee in all thy pride of merit,
Allow'd my Fathers Contract, and did give thee
My Sisters heart in thy own vote, but when,
She onely made a pause for ceremony,
Not disaffection, since thou could'st forget
Thy honour of a Prince, to invade her Chastity,
And forfeit thy Religion, thus I come,
To whip thy blood, or leave my own a sacrifice.

[Enter **PETRONIO**.

Sir, may a stranger ask without offence, why
The Court like Ianus doth present a double
Face, as it labour'd twixt the fierce extremes
Of triumph and despair?

PETRONIO
Sir you mistake not
The mixture of our passions, the Court
Smiles in our happiness to entertain
The Prince, and his fair Mistris, but doth wear,
A grief and paleness, for the Duke, whose want
Of health delayes their marriage.

HONORIO
I apprehend;
Sir I am bold, May not a Gentleman

Engag'd to visit other Courts of Italy,
Make his ambition fortunate to receive
A favour from this Prince, and kiss his hand,
Before he leave the Dukedome?

[Enter **LEONATA**.

PETRONIO
He is here Sir.

LEONATO
Lord Petronia, intreat the Princess
Fioretta, and my Sister meet me i'th' grove—
This Gentleman—

[**HONORIO** kisses his hand.

HONORIO
You have made me happy;
Though I want honor to be known, your fame
Speaks you a valiant Prince, and fortunate,
And I must with the World congratulate
Your victory at Mantua, upon which,
So rich a triumph waites.

LEONATO
What triumph fir?

HONORIO
The Princess Fioretta.

LEONATO
I acknowledge,
That Garland is my glory, such a treasure,
Was worth more service, than my sword could merit:
But I must be a debtor to my starres,
And can release all other happiness,
Within their influence to come, so they
Confirm me Lord still of her beauties Empire.

HONORIO
This doth becom your Excellence; what error
(Receive it not prophane) should Heaven and nature,
Have made, to have kept your hearts too long asunder?
And yet I may mistake, for though your Grace,
Affect her with all height your soul can fancie,
I know not how her love may answer this
Desert in you.

LEONATO
How sir?

HONORIO
Your Highness pardon;
I am no Prophet, nor do wish to see,
Upon your spring, another winde than what
The wings of pregnant Western gales do inrich
The air withall, which gliding as you walk,
May kiss the teeming flowers, and with soft breath
Open the Buds to welcom their preserver;
I wish you might grow up two even Cedars,
Till your top-boughs kiss Heaven that made you flourish,
When stooping to behold the numerous branches
That prosper in your growth, and what refreshing
The World below receives by your cool shade,
You wave your heads in the applause and wonder.
This is the Song I bring to your chast Hymen,
And thus would every good man pray, but that
They fear.

LEONATO
Fear, what?

HONORIO
The blessings they invoke,
With all their importunity of prayers,
Will not descend.

LEONATO
I cannot reach you sir
Without a perspective, but this wanders from
The doubt you made of Fiorettas love,
To answer mine, that talk was dangerous,
I must not hear't agen.

HONORIO
You must, unless
You can be deaf, or cut the tongue of fame out.

LEONATO
The man hath somwhere lost his senses; go back
And sind thy strangled wits, this language has
No chain of reason, I lose breath upon
A thing distracted.

HONORIO

'Tis not come to that,
I've no such hot vexation, but a soul
Possest with noble anger, and with pitty.
Prince, I must tell you there are dangerous symptoms
Of a State Apoplex; those aiery stilts
Of fame you walk on, will deceive your pride,
When every honest breath, angry at what
You did so late in the contempt of goodness,
Will tell the wind how it mistook your praise,
And in a sigh conclude her sad repentance.
I come not sir to flatter.

LEONATO
It appears so.

HONORIO
But tell you what hath eat into your soul
Of honor, and there poisond all the worth
The World once lov'd you for.

LEONATO
You talk as if
You had consulted with my fate, and read
The leaves of my inevitable doom;
What action hath so much incens'd my late
Kind starres to this revolt, and threatneth like
To busie tongues in my disgrace?

HONORIO
The noise is lowd already, would there were
No truth in men, who say, you ravish'd Fioretta
Sweet Princess from her Prayers, and left a Monument
Of such a sacrilege committed by you,
The very stones since groan in her behalf
You ravish'd from the Nunnery, on this
Must needs depend her hate,
Whose person and Religious vow you have
Unlike a Prince prophan'd.

LEONATO
Y'are very bold,
What confidence can that outside raise in you
To be thus sawcie?

HONORIO
Sawcie?

LEONATO

Impudent.
Is life a burden, that you dare my anger?
What art?

HONORIO
A gentleman, that have more right to honor
Than he that is a Prince, and dares degenerate.

LEONATO
There's somthing in thy face would have me think
Thou maist be worth my punishment, that I
Could uncreate thee, if thy veines do house
But Common blood, to make thee a fit Enemy
In Birth, and soul to me, that I might kill thee
Without a blush to honor, do not tempt
My Just rage, that provok'd will scorn a sword,
And make thee nothing with a look; be gone,
Get hence with the same speed, thou wouldst avoid
A falling Tower, or hadst new seen a Lioness
Walking upon some cliff, and gazing round
To find a prey, which she persues with eyes
That shoot contracted flame, but when her teeth
And pawes arrive, they quickly leave no part
Or sign of what there was.

HONORIO
Just heaven, how high he talks, and counterfeits
Your noise! I have a charm against your thunder;
If thou hast courage to stay, thou quickly shalt repent
Heavens Iustice in my arm sent to revenge
Thy sacrilege, the more to encourage thee
To fight, I am thy equall, and a Prince.

[They Draw

Or may thy sin o'take my blood, and set
A weight upon my soul when thou hast kil'd me

[They fight.

[Enter **DONABELLA, JULIANA.**

JULIANA
Alas my Lord?

DONABELLA
Dear Brother?
Help, what traitor's this?

LEONATO
Away sweet Fioretta.

HONORIO
Fioretta.

JULIANA
Ha! I am undone, alas what do you mean?
My Brother, Prince Honorio.

LEONATO
Thy brother?

JULIANA
Oh let me hold thee safe in my Embraces.

DONABELLA, LEONATO
Honorio!

HONORIO
The same, but not her brother.

LEONATO
Pardon me,
Whose soul disdain'd in my belief thou wert
An insolent stranger, to acknowledge any thing
Of satisfaction, but let thy sister
Now speak for both.

HONORIO
Give space to my amazement.

JULIANA
If changing thus soft kisses, armes and heart
You interpret violence, Fioretta, then
Thy sister has been ravished; who hath thus
Abus'd your faith, and wrong'd this Princes Virtue?
Clear as the light of stars. I must confess
I seem'd to wave his courtship, when he first
Beheld me veild, which modesty instructed,
And though my heart were won, I kept it secret,
To make more proof of his, who not consenting
To be depriv'd too long of what he lov'd,
He brought a force to' th' Cloister: but took me
His own away without a rape, and since
All his addresses have been honorable.

HONORIO
Instead of satisfaction, you inlarge
My wonder, what Impostures here? the Prince
Is cosend, yet she ownes me; pardon sir,
I was made believe, you did most impiously
Compell my sister, and by force injoy'd her,
But now I find we are all abus'd, to what
Misfortune might this error have engag'd us?

LEONATO
This is my sister.

HONORIO
You cannot want a charity
That are so fair.

JULIANA
Would Leonato's Sword
Had prosper'd in his death; I must be confident;
You have not yet made glad my heart Honorio,
With our good Fathers health, I have some trembling
Within my blood, and fear all is not well.

HONORIO
Gypsye?

JULIANA
You look not cherefully.

HONORIO
My Father injoyes a perfect health.

JULIANA
That word hath blest me.
Sister and Leonato, you'l excuse,
If I transgress with joy to see my Brother;
Were but the Duke my Father here, I summ'd
All my delights on earth—

HONORIO [aside]
She confounds me.

JULIANA
Honorio and I will follow you.

[Exit **LEONATO** and **DONATELLA**.

HONORIO

You are not my Sister?

JULIANA
Sir, tis very true.

HONORIO
Where is she?

JULIANA
You shall know what will make you happy sir,
If you preserve this wisedom.

HONORIO
I have seen you before.

JULIANA
But I am destin'd here, to do such service
To your Family you shall know more—

HONORIO
Give me breath for two minutes,
Be confident of my silence, they expect you.

[Exit **JULIANA.**

So let me have some air, am I Honorio.

[Enter **FIORETTA** and **BERTOLDI**

What prodigies are these? we are all bewitch'd,
Ha! Sister!

FIORETTA
Brother Honorio.

HONORIO
Tis she, what's he?

FIORETTA
Not worth the interruption of one kiss.

BERTOLDI
My friend—

HONORIO
My fool—Fioretta shew me where
We may injoy a shade, I'l tell thee wonders.

Exeunt **FIORETTA** and **HONORIO**.

BERTOLDI
Sir I shall meet with you agen; a pretty fellow!

[Exit.

ACT IV

SCENE I

A Park.

Enter **FIORETTA** and **DONABELLA**.

FIORETTA
Madam I fear this walk into the Park,
May engage your grace too far without som more
To attend you,

DONABELLA
Our own thoughts may be our guard,
I use it frequently; but to our dlscourse
Of Prince Honorio, for we cannot find
A nobler subject, I observe that he
And you have been aquainted.

FIORETTA
Twas my happiness,
To have my breeding in the Court of Mantua,
Where I among the rest of his admirers,
Seeing his youth improv'd with so much honor,
Grew into admiration of his virtues,
Which now he writes man do so fully crown him,
His Fathers Dukedome holds no ornament
To stand in competition.

DONABELLA
You speak him high,
And with a passion too, that tasts of love.

FIORETTA
Madam, I honor him,
As may become his servant.

DONABELLA

As his Mistris rather.

FIORETTA
My heart is clear from such ambition,

DONABELLA
But yet not proof against all Cupids shaft's;
I do not think but you have been in love.

FIORETTA
Who hath not felt the wounds? but I ne'r look'd
Above my birth and fortunes; Prince Honorio,
May become your election, and great blood.

DONABELLA
I find it here already.

FIORETTA
Nor could you
Endear it where so much desert invites
It to be belov'd.

DONABELLA
My looks do sure betray me,
I do believe him all compos'd of honor,
And have receiv'd your Character from the World
So noble, all your praise can be no flattery.
I know not by what powerfull charm within
His person, Madam, I confess my eyes
Take some delight to see him, but I fear—

FIORETTA
I find your Jealousie, and dare secure you.
If in your amorous bosom, you feel, Madam,
A Golden shaft, the cure is made by cherishing
The happy wound; my destiny hath plac'd
My thoughts of love, where they cannot concern
Your trouble or suspition, nor indeed
My hope, for I despair ever to meet,
His clear affection whom I honour.

DONABELLA
Would
This Court contain'd whom you would make so precious;
I should with as much cherefullness assist
Thy wishes, as desire thy aid to mine;
I do believe you have much credit with
His thoughts, and virtue to deserve it Madam,

FIORETTA

If you trust me,
The favor I have with his Highness, shall not
Create your prejudice, be confident,
Your birth, your beauty, and those numerous graces
That wait upon you, must command his heart.

DONABELLA

Madam you force a blush for my much want
Of what y' are pleas'd to impute my ornaments,
You are acquainted with your self, and shew
What I should be, if I were rich like you,
But my disparity of worth allow'd,
Would you would call me Sister, and impose
Something on me, my act of confidence,
And free discovery of my soul, may
Deserve faith from you, that I shall never
Injure his name you love.

FIORETTA

There is no hope
In my desires, and therefore I beseech,
Dear Madam, your excuse, yet thus much I
Dare borrow of my grief to say, he lives
Now in the Court, for whose sake I thus wither.

DONABELLA

Alas I fear agen, is he compos'd
Of gentle blood, and can to thee he cruell?

FIORETTA

No, he is very kind, for he did promise
To be my Husband, we ha' been contracted.

DONABELLA

Disperse these mists, & clear my wonder Madam.

FIORETTA

When time and sorrow shall by death prepare
My sad release of love, you may know all;
Were the condition of my face like others,
It were no grief to name him.

DONABELLA

This doth more inlarge my Jealousie.

FIORETTA

But let us leave this subject, till time fit,
To ope the maze of my unhappy fortune.

[Exeunt.

SCENE II

Another Part of the Same.

Enter **BERTOLDI**.

BERTOLDI
I heard that she was come into the Park,
They cannot far be; they are in view,
And no man with'em, I'l now be valiant.

[Enter **FLORELIA** and **HONORIO**.

FLORELIA
It was her Highness charge I should direct you,
I know her walk.

BERTOLDI
The blustering Prince agen;
Who sent him hither? I think he conjures.
Now dare I with as much confidence undertake
To cure a Lyon rampant, o' the' Tooth-ach,
As but go forward; and my valiant Mother—

HONORIO
Your Son; I must excuse my self then to him.

BERTOLDI
Now shall I be fit for a Carbonado.

HONORIO
I hope you'l pardon sir, if I appear'd,
Less smooth when I last saw you.

BERTOLDI
My good Lord; your Grace is too much humble,
I'm your blow-ball, your breath dissolves my being,
But to shew how free my wishes are to serve you,
If you have any mind, or meaning to my Mother—

HONORIO

How do you mean?

BERTOLDI
In what way your Grace pleases,
She shall be yours, your Highness may do worse,
Although I say't she has those things may give
A Prince content.

HONORIO
Your Son is very curteous.

FLORELIA
I should prepare you sir to look with mercy
Upon his folly. But the Princess.

BERTOLDI
Mother.

FLORELIA
Will you be still a fool,
What said you sir to th' Prince?

BERTOLDI
Will you be wise and use him tenderly.

FLORELIA
Stain to thy Fathers blood—
I was coming Madam.

[Exeunt **FLORELIA** and **HONORIO**.

BERTOLDI
Umph! he is my rivall, would my hilts
Were in his belly; they are out of sight;
It is no rutting time, no trick?

[Enter **FLAVIANO** and **CLAUDIO** disguis'd.

FLAVIANO
Signior Bertoldi.

BERTOLDI
I do not know you friends, but how soever,
There is a purse of mony

FLAVIANO
Sir, I want not.

BERTOLDI

That Gentleman perhaps can drink; I like not
Their goggle eyes, twas well I gave 'em mony:
What d'ee want else? you are Souldiers;
I love a Souldier.

FLORELIA

I am a Gentleman of Mantua sir,
That owe my life to your command, as one,
That had an interest in the preservation,
Your army brought when the Enemy besieg'd us.

BERTOLDI

Your mercy Signior, and how do all
Our limber friends 'it 'h Nunnery? I was one
O'th' Cavaliers went with the Generall,
Into the Orchard of Hesperides
To fetch the golden Dragon.

FLAVIANO

Golden Apple,
You mean the Princess Fioretta Signior;
Is she married sir?

BERTOLDI

No, no, the Duke will neither dye, nor live,
To any purpose, but they will be shortly;
Have you a mind to kiss her hand?

FLAVIANO

I shall be proud—

BERTOLDI

You shall be as proud as you please sir.

FLAVIANO

You can resolve me, is Honorio
Our Duke of Mantuas Son here?

BERTOLDI

Yes, he is here,
Heaven were a fitter place for him.

FLAVIANO

Ha! look to him,
For he is come with bloody thoughts to murder
Your Prince Leonato, caution him to walk
With a strong guard, and arm himself with all

That can be proof against his Sword or Pistoll,
He cannot be too safe against the treason
And horrid purpose of Honorio.

BERTOLDI
His mouth is Musket bore; but are you sure
He did resolve to kill our Prince?

FLAVIANO
Most certain.

BERTOLDI
I am very glad to hear't.

FLAVIANO
Glad sir?

BERTOLDI
Yes, I cannot wish him better then a Traitor,
Now I shall be reveng'd.

FLAVIANO
Has he been guilty of any affront to you?

BERTOLDI
He is my Rivall.

FLAVIANO
Why do not you kill him then?

BERTOLDI
Pox on him, I cannot indure him.

FLAVIANO
He is then reserv'd to fall by me.

BERTOLDI
Tis too good to be true; are you maryed Signior?

FLAVIANO
What then?

BERTOLDI
If you be not, do this & you shall have
My mother, a Lady that has Gold enough to pave
The Streets with double Ducats, heres my hand,
Kill but this huffing Prince, my Mothers yours,

[Enter **HONORIO**.

And all her moveables—tis he alone too,
There's convenient bottom sir hard by
The finest place to cut his throat, I'l not
Be seen.

FLAVIANO
I am resolv'd, charge home thy litle Murderers,
And follow.

CLAUDIO
I warrant you my Lord.

[Exit after **HONORIO**.

SCENE III

Another Part of the Same.

[Enter **VOLTERINO** and **HORTENSIO**.

VOLTERINO
But tell me hast thou any hopes of Madam Florelia?

HORTENSIO
I had a lusty promise.

VOLTERINO
From her?

HORTENSIO
Ye Coxcomb her sweet Son.

VOLTERINO
Why so had I, he did contract her to me,
A flat bargain and sale of all she had,
So I would say he was valiant.

HORTENSIO
That was the price he made to me, but I,
Had hope last visit from her self.

VOLTERINO
Be plain, I'l tell thee, she gave me strong expectation,
And came on like a Cheverell.

HORTENSIO
I hear,
She has given out she will have one of us,

[Enter **FLORELIA** behind.

VOLTERINO
She cannot love us both.

HORTENSIO
Would she had one! & then the toy were over,
I could make shift to love her.

VOLTERINO
And to lye with her estate, one helps the tother well.

FLORELIA
I finde a change within my self, I hope,
I sha'not prove in love now after all
My jeasting, and so many coy repulses,
To men of birth and honour.

VOLTERINO
Tis she.

FLORELIA
Why do I think upon him, then? I fear,
This man of War has don't.

HORTENSIO
I have it, wee'l finde whether she affect
Or Juggle with us presently.

FLORELIA
Those postures,
Would shew some difference, here I can observe—

VOLTERINO
Your Mistris?

HORTENSIO
Mine if she be pleas'd, what interest
Can all your merit challenge above me?

VOLTERINO
You will repent this insolence, I must,
Forget to wear a sword, and hear thee name

Florelia, with that confident relation
To her fair thoughts, and not correct your pride,
I'l search your heart, and let out those proud hopes,
That thus exalt you.

HORTENSIO
You are cozen'd Signior,
I do not fear your probe—

[They fight.

—she lets us fight,
If we had no more wit, we might foin in earnest.

FLORELIA
Ha, ha, ha! are you at that ward Gentlemen?

VOLTERINO
She laughes to see us fence o' this fashion,
Lets come a little closer.

[They fight.

FLORELIA
Hold, hold Gentlemen,
For your own honors, is this valour well
Employ'd? what cause can urge effusion,
Thus of that noble blood was given you
To serve your Country? are you mad?

HORTENSIO
We are but little better to be both in love.

FLORELIA
What Woman,
Considered in her best is worth this difference;
She is cruel cannot find a better way
To reconcile you, than by letting blood.
Do you both love one?

VOLTERINO
It does appear so Madam.

FLORELIA
I would I knew the Lady makes you both
Unhappy, I would counsell her some way,
To set your hearts at peace.

VOLTERINO

Tis in your power.

HORTENSIO

Without more circumstance, do but look upon
Your self, and end our civill Wars; we ha' both
Opinion of your virtue, and both hope
An interest in your love, if you will please
To point which of us two is most concern'd
In your affection, you conclude our danger,
And oblige one your everlasting Servant.

VOLTERINO

This Madam is a charitable way
To know your own, and save two lives, for we
Shall fix upon your sentence, and obey
The fate you give us.

FLORELIA

Do you fight for me?
And will it save incision and preserve
Your noble veins to know whom I prefer
In my best thoughts of love? this is but reasonable,
And twill be hard to set a period
To this contention, for I love you both
So equally, observe me Cavaliers,
Tis most impossible to distinguish which
Is first in my neglect, for I love neither:
Fight or be friends, you have your choice, and I
My liberty—I had forgot to thank you,
For your infusion of that fierce courage
Into my Son, there is great hope if he
Live till next year, he may be a Constable,
He has an excellent art to keep the peace.
Farewell!

[Going.

VOLTERINO

Madam, for all this I believe you love—

HORTENSIO

I believe now shee's old and has no teeth,
Else she would bite at one of us—Reverend Madam,
That word has fetch'd her,—we ha' no other cordiall,
At this dead pang for your disdain, but drink now;
If you will have your Son made a fine Gentleman,
Be sure you send him to the Tavern to us,

He knows the rendezvous, though you despair,
We may wind him up yet with spirit of Wine,
How ever wee'l be merry, and perhaps,
For all this, drink your health.

VOLTERINO
Bye, Madam.

HORTENSIO
If you love your Baby send him.

[Exeunt **VOLTERINO** and **HORTENSIO**.

FLORELIA
I am to blame, but I must help it some way.

[Exit.

SCENE IV

Another Part of the Park.

Enter **HONORIO**, **FLAVIANO**, **CLAUDIO** with Pistols.

HONORIO
Two Engins of so small extent to do
Such mighty execution? may I see
These instruments you say you have invented,
And so commend for service?

FLAVIANO
Yes my Lord,
Shew 'em to th' Prince, do they not fright already?
Your Grace may take full view, and quickly be
The proof what force they have.

HONORIO
I am betrai'd,
Who hath conspir'd my death

FLAVIANO
To vex you, see him—

[Discovers himself.

HONORIO

Flaviano, what mak'st thou here?

FLAVIANO

To put of these commodities; you are
A princely Marchant, and affect this kind
Of traffick, that you may not dy i'th' dark,
I'l tell you a brief story, which you may
Report i'th' other world, I did affect
Ambitiously thy Sister Fioretta,
Abus'd thy Father with a false opinion
Of Leonato, for my end remov'd
His Mistris from the Cloister, and perswaded
A witty Nunne to take her name, and cheat
The Prince, whom he suspects not yet.

HONORIO

Dam'd rascall?

FLAVIANO

For pure love to your Sister I did this.

HONORIO

Why having been so impious, does thy malice
Persue me, ignorant of all thy treasons?

FLAVIANO

Would you know that?—because I am undone
In my chief hope, the Princess whom I thought
Thus plac'd secure, and apt for my own visit
Is gone, is vanish'd, and as soon I may
Find the impression of a Ship at Sea,
And by the hollow tract in waves oretake
The winged Bark, distinguish where the Birds,
At Chace 'ith' air, do print their active flight,
As find in what part of the envious World
Fioretta is bestow'd; this sad intelligence
Surpriz'd me like a storm, nor was it safe
To look upon the Duke, who must too late
Repent his trust, and punish it. In this conflict
Of desperate thoughts, I thus resolv'd to see
Ferrara, and the Lady I preferr'd,
But find things cannot prosper, if you live?
Whose angry breath will throw down waht my policy
Wrought high, and strike my head beneath the ruines.
Are you now satisfi'd why you must not live?

HONORIO

Hear me, shee's still in silence, and believ'd

My Sister by the Prince.

FLAVIANO
When you are dead, then
You Will be sure to tell no tales; now shoot—

CLAUDIO
In my opinion, if all this be truth,
The mischief you ha' done may be sufficient,
And he may live.

FLAVIANO
Villain wilt thou betray me?

CLAUDIO
You have betraid your self, and after this
Confession, as I take it, I may be
Your Ghostly Father, and prescribe you a Penance.

[Points the pistol at him.

FLAVIANO
Hold!

CLAUDIO
I will but Physick you, your soul has caught
A vehement cold, and I have two hot pills
Will warm you at heart.

HONORIO
Shall my revenge be idle?

[Draws his sword.

CLAUDIO
Good Prince, you are too forward, & you be
So hasty, I'm o' this side; did you think,
I would be false? yet lest my aim be unlucky,
Trust your own hand to guide 'em.

[Gives the pistols to **FLAVIANO**.

FLAVIANO
Thou art honest,
Thus I salute thy heart Honorio—

[Snaps the pistol at **HONORIO**.

Ha! no charge.

CLAUDIO
Tis time sir to be honest, I could serve you
In some Court sins, that are but flesh-colour,
A wickedness of the first dye, whose brightness
Will fade, and tincture change; your murder is
Crimson in grain, I have no fancy too't.
Sir you are safe.

HONORIO
I see thou hast preserv'd me.

FLAVIANO
I'm lost for ever.

HONORIO
'Tis but a minute
Since you were found, you must be pleas'd to walk
Into the Court, the Vestall you preferr'd
No doubt will bid you welcome. Fate I thank thee.

FLAVIANO
False starres, I dare you now.

CLAUDIO
I shall wait on you.

[Exeunt.

SCENE V

An Apartment in the Palace.

Enter **JULIANA**.

JULIANA
I have collected all my brain, and cannot
In any counsell of my thoughts find safety;
Honorio's death wo'not secure my strength,
Or prop my languishing greatness; tis but like
A cordiall when the pangs of death hang on us,
Nay to my present state no other than
Some liberall portion of a quivering stream,
Drunk to abate the scorching of my Feaver,
It cooles to'th' tast, and creeps like Ice dissolv'd

Into my blood, but meeting with the flame,
It scalds my bosom, and augments the fire
That turnes my heart to ashes; poor Juliana,
To what a loss hath thy first sin betray'd thee!
Ambition hath reveng'd thy breach of Honor,
And Death must cure Ambition, for I have
No prospect left, but what invites to ruine.
I am resolv'd not to expect my fate,
But meet it this way.

[Shews a poniard.

[Enter **LEONATO**.

LEONATO
Dearest Fioretta?
Ha, what offends my Princess? there is something
That dwells like an Ecclipse upon thy eyes,
They shine not as they did, a discontent,
Is like a mildew fallen upon thy cheek,
Tis pale and cold, as Winter were come back
To over-run the Spring.

JULIANA
My dearest Lord,
My face is but the title to a volume
Of so much misery within, as will
Tire your amazed soul to read.

LEONATO
Thou dost
Freeze up my blood already. O call back
Part of this killing language, if thou mean'st
To make me understand thee; the amazement
Doth fall so like a deluge, I am drownd,
Ere I can think my feares; how have we liv'd
At distance? thou shouldst walk upon this Earthquake
And my ground tremble not, but with this fright
I am awake, open the volume now,
I will read every circumstance.

JULIANA
Observe then, what first becomes my sorrow.

[Kneels.

LEONATO
Dost thou kneel?

That posture is for them have lost their Innocence;
We must do this to Heaven.

JULIANA
I must to you.

LEONATO
What guilt can weigh thee down so low?
Dost weep too!

JULIANA
I should not love my eyes if they were silent,
They know this story will too soon o'rcharge
My feeble voice, that every tear could fall
Into some character which you might read,
That so I might dispense with my sad tongue,
And leave my sorrows legible; oh my Lord,
I have wrong'd you above hope to find your mercy.

LEONATO
Take heed, & think once more what thou hast don
Ere thou describe such an offence, lest I
Believe a fault, will drown us both with horror;
Thou hast not broke thy vows nor given away
Thy honor, since thy faith did seal thee mine?

JULIANA
Not in a thought.

LEONATO
I wo'not see thee kneel,
Rise, and be welcome to my armes, thou hast
Done nothing can offend me Fioretta.

JULIANA
Alas—I am not Fioretta.

LEONATO
Ha! this doth confirm me, thou hast all this while
But mock'd my fear, and yet this weeping is
Not counterfeit, thou art too blame my love,
Is it thy jealousie, that I am cold
In my returnes to answer thy affection?
Or have I less in thy esteem of merit
Than thy hopes flatterd thee? or doth the time
That dully moves, and intermit the joyes
We promis'd when the Altar had confirm'd us
Sit heavy on thy thought? we will awake

From this our sullen sleep, and quit off those
Sick Feathers that did droop our wings; fly to
The holy man whose charm shall perfect us,
And chain our amorous soules.

JULIANA
Divide us rather;
Joy is a fugitive of late, and while
You think of Hymen, you remove your wishes.
Fioretta will forbid the Priest.

LEONATO
Canst thou forget thy love so much?

JULIANA
Alas my Lord,
You have been all this while abus'd, and when
I have said enough to assure your Faith, that I
Am not your Fioretta, but a Virgin,
Compell'd to take her name, you will I hope
Kill me your self, and save me a despair,
That will conclude my breath else in few Minutes.

LEONATO
Are not you Fioretta, but a Virgin
Compell'd to take her name? who durst compell thee?

JULIANA
The Duke of Mantua.

LEONATO
I dissolve in wonder.
Durst Mantua use me thus? thy name?

JULIANA
Juliana;
My blood, (excepting what does fill the veins
Of Princes) flowing from the noblest spring
Of honour.

LEONATO
Where was Fioretta then?

JULIANA
Convey'd I know not whither, ere you came
To save their lives that did betray you thus.
I was too careless of my fate, that I
Kept such a glowing secret still within me,

I had no fear to be consum'd, that had
Another Fire within me, whose wide flame
Had soon devour'd all my considerings.
Alas my Lord, You did appear so full
Of honor, virtue, and such Princely love,
Twas easie to forget on whom you smil'd,
I had no thought to wish my self unhappy,
Or own another name to my undoing,
Yet now more tender of your birth and fame
Than my own life, I cast my self beneath
Your feet a bleeding sacrifice.

LEONATO
Am I awake and hear all this?

JULIANA
I see my Lord,
In your inraged eye, what lightning is
Prepar'd, tis welcom; since I danot hope
To live upon your smile, I would fain dye
Betime, before the shame of my dishonour
Inforce a mutinie upon my self.
But think my Lord while I confess all this
Against my self, how free I might have been,
How happy, how near Heaven, above those glories,
Had not you forc'd me from the blessed Garden
Where I was planted, and grew fair, though not
Oblig'd by any solemn vow, 'twas you,
Your own hand ravish'd me from that sweet life,
Where without thought of more than should concern
Your welfare in my prayers, I might have sung,
And had converse with Angels.

[Enter **PETRONIO**.

PETRONIO
Sir, I bring sad news.

LEONATO
I prethee speak, I am prepar'd for all.
PETRONIO
The Duke is dead.

LEONATO
My Father dead?

PETRONIO
I do not like the Princess at that posture.

LEONATO
I have forgot your name Lady—you may rise.

[Enter **HONORIO**, **FLAVIANO**, **CLAUDIO** and **GUARD**.

HONORIO
My Lord I bring you news welcom as health
Or liberty, your soul will not be spacious
Enough to entertain what will with joyes
And strong amazement fill it; how I swell,
With my own happiness to think I shall
Redeem your noble heart from a dishonor
Wil weigh down death. You think you walk on Roses
And feel not to what Dragons teeth, and stings,
You were betraid. I bring a disinchantment,
And come with happy proofs.

LEONATO
To tell me this is not
Your Sister Fioretta: but a Nunne
Subornd to cheat me—I know all the business,
And am resolv'd in my revenge. Juliana,
Sweet suffering Maid, dry thy fair eyes, tis I
Must make thee satisfaction, I thus
By thy own name receive thee to my bosom,
But you that practis'd cunning, shall e'r time
Contract the age of one pale Moon, behold
The Countrey I preserv'd a heap of ruines.

JULIANA
Flaviano? [aside] sir—

HONORIO
Do you know whom you embrace?
Flaviano has confest
Himself the Traitor, and the black contriver
Of all this mischief; Leonato hear me,
Or by thy Father newly falln to ashes,
I shall repent I had an honorable
Thought of thee. Flaviano; Madam, witchcraft,
My rage will strangle my discourse, my soul
Is leaping forth to be reveng'd upon
That Devill; Prince keep off, his very breath
Will stifle thee, and dam thy honor to
All ages. Fioretta's now in Court.

FLAVIANO

Ha! in the Court?

LEONATO
This is some new device.

HONORIO
I charge thee by thy blood throw of these Harpies,
And do my Sister justice, whom their treason
Hath made a scorn, that minute she usurps
Her name of Bride, I shall forget the Altar,
And turn my self the Priest, with all your blood
To make a purging sacrifice.

LEONATO
If when we
Receive our rites, thou dost but frown, or whisper
To interrupt one ceremony, I
Will make thee hold the tapers while the Priest
Performes the holy office; tell thy Sister
Here I bestow, what you have made me forfeit.
Present her to the Nunnery, and counsell
Thy ignoble Father, when I next see Mantua
To be a sleep in's Coffin, and his vault
Deep, and thick rib'd with Marble, my noise else
Will shake his dust; thy youth finds mercy yet,
Take the next whirl-wind, and remove—our guard;
Petronio we confine him to your house.

HONORIO
Thou coward Prince, there's not one honest man
In all the World, our sins ascend like vapours,
And will, if Justice sleep, stupifie Heaven,
For thine own glory wake, if thou dispense
With this, proud man will cry down providence.

[Exeunt.

ACT V

SCENE I

A Tavern. A Table and Stools Set Out.

Enter **VOLTERINO, HORTENSIO, PANDOLPHO** with a towel.

VOLTERINO

Such Wine as Ganimede doth skink to Iove
When he invites the Gods to feast with him
On Junos wedding-day.

PANDOLPHO
Jove never drank so brisk a Nectar as I'l draw.
But does Signior Bertoldi come?

HORTENSIO
What else? my Alderman o'th' Cellar.

VOLTERINO
He is our Hilas; shall we not ha Musick?

HORTENSIO
By all means, and the Mermaids.

PANDOLPHO
You shall have any thing;
But if Signior Bertoldi come, I have
A boon to beg, I have a pretty plot
To make you laugh.

VOLTERINO
What is't?

PANDOLPHO
As you are Gentlemen, do not deny me;
I have been your up-and-down-stairs-man to draw
The best blood o'th' Grape these ten years,
Troy held out not longer, I have a device
Shall make you merry when he comes, if you
Will give me leave to shift, and help a jest.
He is a Coward still, under the Rose?

HORTENSIO
As any lives under the Sun, be confident.

VOLTERINO
The same senseless piece of timber,
You may cut him into a Bed-staff.

PANDOLPHO
I'l send you Wine, say I am valiant,
Let me alone with the Catastrophe.

[Exit

HORTENSIO
What will he do?

VOLTERINO
I know not, he were best make us laugh,
I shall expound the matter else.

[Enter **BERTOLDI** and **SERVANT** with Wine.

BERTOLDI
My Mother remembers her service Gentlemen,
I left my Mistris to come to you; and how?
Shall we drink like Fishes? Tolle roll lolly, &c.

VOLTERINO
Sit, sit, a health to the Lady you kist last.

[Drinks.

BERTOLDI
Let it come, I'l pledge it,
And it were the Gulf of Venice.

[Drinks.

HORTENSIO
And who's your Mistris?

BERTOLDI
Faith I do not know her name, nor ever kist any thing but her Glove in my life.

VOLTERINO
But you have told her your mind?

BERTOLDI
Not I by this Wine—but thats all one,
She is a Lady, well bred, and companion
To the Princess, that's enough.
Here Signior—would we had some Wenches here.

HORTENSIO
Some bouncing bona robas, hang this dul City there's no musick in't, no silken Musick.

VOLTERINO
Oh for a Wench could spit fire now, that could whizze like a Rocket, and fall into a 100 blasing stars, such a Fire-drake would be warm company in a close room, Signior.

HORTENSIO

And it were in a Cellar under the Alpes, it would make Hercules melt in the back.

BERTOLDI
But for all that, I do not like a sinner of such a fiery constitution.

HORTENSIO
You would not venture upon the golden Fleece then, which is but the morall of a Maidenhead.

BERTOLDI
I never heard that afore.

HORTENSIO
So say the learned, first for the difficulty to obtain it, being watch'd by a Dragon, and then for the Rarity, there being but one in all the World.

BERTOLDI
But one Maidenhead?

VOLTERINO
And that some hold as doubtfull as the Phoenix or Unicorn, such things are in History, but the man's not alive that will take his Oath in what climat they are visible. Here's to the Swan that broke her heart with singing last.

HORTENSIO
And to the Dolphin that was in love with a Fidlers Boy of Thebes, who carryed him cross the Seas on her bak a fishing, while he sung the siege of Troy to the Tune of Green-sleeves, and caught a Whale with an angling rod.

[Drinks.

BERTOLDI
I'l pledge 'em both; they are very fine healths.

[Drinks.

Are these your Mistresses names Gentlemen?

[Enter **PANDOLPHO** like a Soldier.

VOLTERINO
Mystical, Mystical.

BERTOLDI
I Understand they are mystical—who's this?

PANDOLPHO
Save you Gentlemen.

VOLTERINO [aside to **HORTENSIO**]
Tis the Drawer.

PANDOLPHO
I do not like the odor of your Wine

[He throws it in **BERTOLDI's** face.

BERTOLDI
Was it a health? let it go round Gent. I am troubled with sore eyes, & this Signior has wash'd 'em for me,
I hope I shall see to thank him.

HORTENSIO
Cry mercy Signior, you are like a noble Gent. I saw at Rome, you are the very same, to whom his Holiness
gave a pension, for killing 6 great Turks in Transilvania, whose heads were boyl'd, and brought home in a
Portmantua.

PANDOLPHO
It was but five sir and a Saracens.

HORTENSIO
You are the man?

VOLTERINO
Pray give me leave to honor you.

BERTOLDI
I desire to be your poor admirer too,
My eyes are clear to see your worth, my name
Is Bertoldi at your service.

PANDOLPHO
To you Signior, a health to Julius Caesar, Prester John,
And the grand Cham of Tartaria.

[Drinks.

VOLTERINO
You sha'not pledge him.

BERTOLDI
No.

VOLTERINO
Make your exceptions, I'l justifie 'em.

HORTENSIO
This Cavalier drank t'ee sir.

BERTOLDI
I do remember, but I cannot pledge him.

PANDOLPHO
How sir?

BERTOLDI
No sir, I'l pledge my friend Prester Iack,
But for Julius Caesar and the grand Cham they are
Pagans, I ha' nothing to say to 'em.

[Enter **SERVANT**.

SERVANT
Here is a Gentleman, he seems of quality,
Enquiring for Signior Volterino and Hortensio.

HORTENSIO
Admit him, and he be a Gentleman.

[Enter **FLORELIA** like a Gentleman.

FLORELIA
You'l pardon if a stranger that has had
A long ambition to kiss your hands,
Rather intreat for his access, than lose
The happiness of your knowledge.

VOLTERINO
Sir, y'are most welcome.

HORTENSIO
If you will keep us company
You must be equally ingag'd.

BERTOLDI
My humble service, Signior Hortensios Mistris!

[Drinks.

FLORELIA
You honor me; would I were off agen.

BERTOLDI
Excuse me Signior.

FLORELIA

Y'are too full of ceremony.

PANDOLPHO
Sir, is there any difference between you & Julius Caesar,
You would not pledge his health?

BERTOLDI
No difference in the world.

PANDOLPHO
How, no difference between you, and a Roman Emperor?

FLORELIA
Divide' em, what's the matter?

HORTENSIO
O for some Trumpets.

BERTOLDI
Somebody hold my Sword, give me the Wine,
I'l drink it—

[Drinks.

PANDOLPHO
So! we are friends.

FLORELIA
O shamefull!

BERTOLDI
But I shall find a time—

PANDOLPHO
Find twenty thousand years, there's time enough.

VOLTERINO
I'l be your stickler.

BERTOLDI
I ha' not pledg'd the Cham yet, nor I wo' not, come, I know you well enough.

PANDOLPHO
Know me, for what?

BERTOLDI
For a brave fellow, and a man may believe thee thou hast done things as well as the best on 'em, but I know not where, nor I care not, tel me of Julius Caesar: I am a Gentleman, and have seen fighting afore

now, here's a Cavalier knows it, I scorn to be baffel'd by any Transilvanian Turk-killer in Christendom, I; thou art a mufti.

VOLTERINO
Well said, and a Sandiack.

BERTOLDI
And a Sandiack, I defie the grand Cham, and Muftie. all his Tartars, y'are a stinking obstreperons fellow to tell me of a Turd and a Fart, and I honor you with all my heart.

HORTENSIO
He call'd you Mufti.

PANDOLPHO
What's that?

HORTENSIO
And a Sandiack, that is son of whor in 2 languages.

PANDOLPHO
How? in two languages? then my honor is
Concern'd, have I in thirty battles gainst the Turk
Stood the dire shock, when the Granadoes flew
Like Atomes in the Sun?
Have I kil'd twenty Bashawes, and a Musselman,
And took the Sultans Turban Prisoner,
And shall I be affronted by a thing
Less than a Lancepresado?

BERTOLDI
Will no body hold me?

FLORELIA
Gentlemen, this heat must needs be dangerous.

PANDOLPHO
Let me but speak with him

VOLTERINO
No danger o' my life, let 'em go together:
And let us mind our business.

PANDOLPHO
Signior, I am your friend, and pitty you
Should lose so much your honor, be advis'd,
I'l show a way how to repair your fame,

[**PANDOLPHO & BERTOLDI** talk privately.

And without danger.

HORTENSIO
To Volterinos Mistris.

[Drinks.

FLORELIA
I receive it, I shall have my share, I now
Repent my curiosity to see
Their humors, and to hear what they would say
Of me—

HORTENSIO
Let 'em alone—to Volterinos Mistris.

[Drinks.

VOLTERINO
Come, to my Whore!

[Drinks.

FLORELIA
Your Whore Signior?

VOLTERINO
Does that offend you?

FLORELIA
Not me—I have done you right.
I am well enough rewarded & they beat me.

BERTOLDI
I know not how to deserve this curtesie being a stranger:
But if you want a Wife noble sir, and will accept of my
Mother, you shall have her before any man in Italy.

PANDOLPHO
I thank you sir,
But be sure you hit me full o'th' head.

BERTOLDI
Tis too much, a cut o'th' leg and please you.

PANDOLPHO
No, let it be o'th' head.

BERTOLDI
You wo'not strike agen?

PANDOLPHO
Mine's but a foil.

HORTENSIO
They measure and give back—

[**BERTOLDI** strikes **PANDOLPHO**.

PANDOLPHO
Oh I am slain, a Surgeon. Bertoldi strikes

FLORELIA
I'l take my leave.

HORTENSIO
By this hand, I'l drink his Mothers health first,
There's no danger & he were dead; a health to the Lady

FLORELIA
I drink it for his sake.

[Drinks.

VOLTERINO
Away, and get a Surgeon.

[Exit **PANDOLPHO**.

BERTOLDI
Come, to my Lady Mother.

[Drinks.

A man is not born to be a coward all his life.

FLORELIA
I can no more sir.

HORTENSIO
You should ha' told me sir at first,
There is no remedy, tis to an honorable Lady.

FLORELIA
You must excuse me sir.

BERTOLDI
Throw't in his eyes.

HORTENSIO
At your request.

[**HORTENSIO** throws the wine in **FLORELIA'S** face.

FLORELIA
Y'are most uncivil.

HORTENSIO
Y'are a mushrump.

[Strikes **FLORELIA**.

FLORELIA
So sir, y'are a multitude, and in a Tavern,
I did believe you sir a Gentleman,
If you be, give me satisfaction nobly.

HORTENSIO
With all my heart.

FLORELIA
Then thus—

[Enter **SERVANT**.

SERVANT
Signior Bertoldi fly, his wound is dangerous,
We fear he will bleed to death before the Surgeon come.

VOLTERINO
Out by the Postern.

BERTOLDI
Pox, a conspiracie, I shall kill but one, I see that;
Would I were a Mite in a Holland Cheese now.

[Exit.

HORTENSIO
I wo'not fail you sir.

SERVANT
He desires to speak with you before he dye.

HORTENSIO
Is Bertoldi gone?

VOLTERINO
Hortensio, I guess you may be ingag'd:
Leave me to these things, There may be danger.

HORTENSIO
I know the private way.

[Exeunt.

A Garden.

[Enter **HONORIO**.

HONORIO
Virtue and honor, I allow you names,
You may give matter for dispute, and noise,
But you have lost your Essence, and that truth
We fondly have believ'd in human soules,
Is ceas'd to be, we are grown fantastick bodies,
Figures, and empty titles, and make hast
To our first nothing, he that will be honest,
Must quite throw off his cold decrepit nature,
And have a new creation—my poor Sister,

[Enter **FIORETTA**.

She has heard the Dukes resolve.

FIORETTA
Oh let me dye, upon thy bosom Brother,
I have liv'd
Too long; they say the Duke resolves to marry
With Juliana, so they call her now,
Whose sorcery hath won upon his soul;
I have walk'd too long in dark Clouds, and accuse
Too late my silence, I am quite undone,
There was some hope while he did love my name,
But that and all is banish'd; is't not in
The power of fancy to imagine this
A dream that hath perplext us all this while?

If it be reall, I will be reveng'd,
Tis but forgetting what I am, and then
I am not concern'd.

HONORIO
Rather forget the Duke,
And live to triumph in a love more happy.
He is not worth a tear.

[Enter **DONABELLA**.

DONABELLA
How's this? my heart!

HONORIO
Come, I wil kiss these sorrows from thy cheek,
This Garden wants no watering, preserve
This rain, it is a wealth should ransom Queens,
As thou dost love me, chide thy saucie grief,
That will undo the spring here, and inforce
My heart to weep within me equall drops
Of blood for these.

DONABELLA
Oh my abus'd confidence,
Lauriana now I find hath but betraid me,
Instruct me rage and jealousie.

FIORETTA
I am resolv'd.

[Exit.

HONORIO
Well said, take courage Fioretta,
Appear with thy own name and sufferings,
Thy sight will strike the proud Impostors from
Their Pyramids of glory.

FIORETTA
It were more revenge to dye.

HONORIO
Not so deer Fioretta, somthing glides
Like cheerfulness o'th' suddrn through my blood;
Despair not to be happy: Let's consult,
And form the aptest way for all our honour.

[Exeunt.

An Apartment in the Palace.

[Enter **FLAVIANO**.

FLAVIANO
There's but one cloud in all our sky, were that
Remov'd, we were above the rage of storms:
That Claudio knows too much. I look upon
His life like a prodigious blazing Comet;
He palls my blood; if I but meet him hansomly,
I'l make him fixt as the North-star. I hear
No whisper of him yet; were but he dead,
Juliana and her friend might revell here:
The Duke should have the name, but we would steer
The Helm of State, and govern all. I have
Gain'd much upon Leonato's easie faith,
Who thinks me innocent, and that only duty
Mislead my nature and my tongue to obey
The Duke of Mantua and the Prince, upon
Whose heads I have translated all my guilt,

[Enter **LEONATO** and **CLAUDIO**.

And fram'd their jealousie at home my cause
Of flight for refuge hither—Ha, my eyes
Take in confusion! The Duke and Claudio!
'Tis doomsday in my soul.

LEONATO
Can this be justified?

CLAUDIO
I dare confirm this truth with my last blood.

FLAVIANO
I dare not hear it. That I now could fling
My self upon the winds—

[Exit.

CLAUDIO
And should be happy

Were Flaviano's life put into ballance
Against my own, to make it clear by his
Confession. To my shame I must acknowledge
I was the agent 'twixt 'em; he was pleas'd
To choose me his smock Officer, a place
Poor Gentlemen at Court are forc'd to serve in,
To please luxurious greatness, younger brothers,
Who cannot live by fair and honest wayes,
Must not sterve sir.

LEONATO
Flaviano's Whore?
Where can we hope to trust our faith, when such
White browes deceive us?

[Enter **JULIANA**.

JULIANA
I do not like
This Claudio's business here, the Duke is troubled;
My whole frame trembles.

LEONATO
Madam Juliana?
My excellent white Devil, you are welcome,
Where is your Catamountain Flaviano?
You are no Serpents spawn?

JULIANA
Oh hear me sir, by your own goodness.

LEONATO
When didst thou kneel to Heaven?

JULIANA
I see my leprosie unveild, that sin
Which with my loss of honor first ingag'd
My miserie, is with a Sun-beam writ
Upon my guilty forehead, but I have not
(Excepting the concealment of my shame,
Which charity might privelege) offended
Above what I confest, and you have pardond.

LEONATO
She hath a tongue would almost tempt a Saint
To unbeleeve Divinity, she learnd
Some accents from the first Apostate Angell
That mutin'd in Heaven; away,

I dare not trust my frailty; where's Flaviano?

[Exit **LEONATO** and **CLAUDIO**.

JULIANA
My soul doth apprehend strange shapes of horror.

[Enter **FIORETTA**.

Ha!—tis the Princess Fioretta.

FIORETTA
Can you direct me Madam, how I may
Speak with the noble Lady Juliana?

JULIANA
I can instruct you Madam where to find
A miserable woman of that name.

FIORETTA
Where?

JULIANA
Here.

[Kneels.

FIORETTA
Do not deceive me,
I came to visit her whom the Dukes love
And confluence of glories must create
A Duchess, to whose greatness I must pay
My adoration.

JULIANA
Do not mock her, Madam,
To whose undoing nothing wants but death;
Let not my sin, which cannot hope your pardon,
Make you forget your virtue; Princely natures,
As they are next to forms Angelical,
Shew the next acts of pity, not derision,
When we are fall'n from Innocence.

FIORETTA
Do you know me?

JULIANA
For the most injur'd Princess, Fioretta.

FIORETTA

You must know more, I come to take revenge
And kill thee.

JULIANA

Thus I kneel to meet your wounds,
And shall account the drops my proud veines weep
Spent for my cure; oh Madam you are not cruell,
You have too soft, too mercifull a look;
When you see me, your countenance should wear
Upon it all the terrors that pale men
Can apprehend from the wild face of War,
A civill War, that wo' not spare the womb
That gron'd and gave it life, this would become you,
Or fancie meager Famine when she hunts
With hollow eyes, and teeth able to grind
A rock of Adamant to dust, or what
Complexion the devouring pest should have,
Were it to take a shape, and when you put
Their horrors in your visage, look on me.

FIORETTA

What hath prepar'd this bold resolve?

JULIANA

A hope
To be your sacrifice; I was not before
Without a thought to wish my self thus layd,
And at your feet to beg you would destroy me.

FIORETTA

Can you so easily consent to dy,
And know not whither afterwards this guilt
Would fling thy wandring soul?

JULIANA

Yes. I would pray
And ask your self, and the wrong'd world forgiveness.

FIORETTA

Why didst thou use me thus?

[Weeps.

JULIANA

I could, if you
Durst hear me, say something perhaps would take

Your charity. Do you weep? gentle Madam?
And not one crimson drop from me, to wait
Upon those precious shewers? not to invite
Your patience upon the lost Juliana,
But to call back your tears into their spring,
And stay the weeping stream, I can inform you,
The Duke looks on me now with eyes of anger;
I have no interest in a thought from him,
That is not arm'd with hate and scorn against me.

FIORETTA
This will undoe my pity, and assure me
Thou hast all this while dissembled with my Justice.

JULIANA
I would I might as soon invest my soul
With my first purity, as clear this truth;
Or would the loss of him were all that sits
Heavy upon my heart; I cannot hope
For comfort in delayes of death, and dare
Attend you to him, though it more undo me.

FIORETTA
Rise, and obey me then.

JULIANA
I follow, Madam;
My use of life is only meant to serve you.

[Exeunt.

SCENE IV

A Wood.

[Enter **HORTENSIO**.

HORTENSIO
This is the place within the wood he promis'd
To meet in, there is Saint Felices Chapell,
That Father Cyprians cell, I hope my Gamster
Will think it fit, I should not walk and wait
Too long for him, these businesses of fighting
Should be dispatch'd as Doctors do prescribe
Physicall Pills, not to be chewd but swallow'd;
Time spent in the considering deads the appetite,

If I were not to fight now, I could pray;
These terms of honor have but little grace with 'em,
Like Oysters we do open one another
Without much preface; he that fights a duell
Like a blind man that falls but cares to keep
His staffe, provides with art to save his honor,
But trusts his soul to chance, tis an ill fashion.

[Enter **FRIAR**.

FRIAR
This is the Gentleman by her description
That comes to fight, another Champion?

[Enter **FLAVIANO**.

FLAVIANO
Do none persue me, what a timerous Hare
This guilty conscience is, I am not safe,
I had no time to think of a disguise,
And this can be no wilderness, the Duke
Would give his Pallace for my head.

HORTENSIO [aside]
Say so?

FLAVIANO
Oh for some Pegasus to mount! a Frier?
His habit will serve rarely, seeming holiness
Is a most excellent shrowd to cheat the world.
Good Father sanctity, I must be bold,
Or cut your throat, nay I can follow.

FRIAR
Help, help.

[Runs off.

HORTENSIO
Thou sacrilegious Villain!

FLAVIANO
I am caught already.

HORTENSIO
My good Lord Flaviano. Father
You may come back, and help to bind the Gentleman
If I did understand him well, he said

The Duke has some affairs to use his head-peece;
I would not have him out o'th' way, when I
Return—to that tree—

[They bind **FLAVIANO** to a tree.

You were best be gentle.

FLAVIANO
I can but dye.

FLAVIANO is tied to a Tree.

HORTENSIO
Oh yes, you may be damn'd
All in good time, and it is very likely.

FRIAR
You have preserv'd my life Son.

HORTENSIO
It was my happiness to be so near,
When virtue was distrest.

FRIAR
You have not done sir,
As you are noble follow me, there is
Another enemy to meet, but I
Dare be your second and direct you.

HORTENSIO
What means the Fryer?
I'l walk and see the worst on't.

[Exeunt all but **FLAVIANO**

[Enter **BERTOLDI**.

BERTOLDI
Oh for a Tenement under ground to hide me!
This wood will hardly do't, if I can lurk
Here but till night; I am furnish'd well with ducats;
Your melancholy mole is happy now,
He fears no Officers, but walks invisible;
Would I were chamber-fellow to a worm,
The Rooks have princely lives that dwell upon
The tops of Trees, the Owls and Bats are Gentlemen,
They fly and fear no warrants, every Hare

Out-runs the Constable, only poor man
By nature slow and full of flegm, must stay,
And stand the cursed Law, I do not think
Tis so much Penance to be hang'd indeed,
As to be thus in fear on't.

FLAVIANO
Sir, look this way.

BERTOLDI
Oh! if I had but the heart of a womans Tailor,
I might run away now.

FLAVIANO
I am rob'd and bound.

BERTOLDI
Umh, are you bound? there's the less danger in you.

FLAVIANO
For charity release me.

BERTOLDI
You are surely bound—whats that?
I hear another whispering o' that side;
Now I sweat all over, I but think
If I were naked, how Maids might gather dew
From every part about me—Tis the wind
Among the leaves. I do not like the Trees
Should lay their heads together o' this fashion.
You are my fast friend still.

FLAVIANO
Signior Bertoldi.

BERTOLDI
Does he name me?
You and the Tree shall grow together now,
I came not hither to be known; some Thief,
Or sturdy rogue; I have heard of these devices
In woods before; should I unbind him now,
Hee'd cut my throat, or rob me for my charity.

FLAVIANO
I am the man for your sake undertook
To kill the Prince your rivall.

BERTOLDI

Did you so? I'l trust you ne'r the sooner;
Well remembred, I'me glad y'are not at leisure;
You that will kill your Prince, will make but little
Conscience to quarter me.

FLAVIANO
But he is still alive.

BERTOLDI
Is he so?
Why then I am the less beholding to you.
So, you shall cancell your own bonds your self.

[Enter **HORTENSIO**, **FLORELIA** and **FRIAR**.

How now, more persecution?

HORTENSIO
Here was a Duell quickly taken up,
And quaintly too, I did not think to marry
The Gentleman that challeng'd me to fight,
I thank your device Madam.

FLORELIA
Thank the blow you gave me sir,
I love a man dares strike.

HORTENSIO
I'l please you better with my after striking.

BERTOLDI
My Mother and Hortensio?

[Enter **VOLTERINO** and **OFFICERS**.

VOLTERINO
Signior Bertoldi well met, lay hands on him
And bind him fast, he has a dangerous spirit

BERTOLDI
Who I? you may as well say I have skil in the
Black art, Volterino, Gentlemen, there's my Mother.

VOLTERINO
Your Son is valiant Madam now I hope,
As you can wish, he has kil'd his man; but I
Studious to gain your favor have procur'd?
His pardon from the Duke.

HORTENSIO
Is the Drawer dead?

VOLTERINO
Dead as the Wine he sometimes drew.

HORTENSIO
Farewell he; will you salute my Lady Signior
And give us joy? yon Frier married us.

BERTOLDI
Let me go, I have my pardon.

VOLTERINO
Not yet; now you shall be hang'd agen,
Did not you swear I should have your Mother?

BERTOLDI
You shall have her yet.

FLORELIA
If it be so,
He shall be worth your suit, and compound fairly.

VOLTERINO
No, I have thought of my revenge; because
I cannot have your Mother, d'ee observe,
If you expect the benefit of this pardon,
You shall marry mine.

BERTOLDI
I'l marry any living soul,

VOLTERINO
Shee's something old, till the last night I see her not
These forty years, since when shee's grown so ugly,
I dare not own her, and some think the reason
Of her deformity to proceed from witchcraft.

BERTOLDI
Alas good Gentlewoman.

VOLTERINO
I mean she is a Witch her self,
And has two Cats they say,
Suck her by turnes, which some call her Familiars;
She has not had a tooth this thirty years;

And you must kiss her with a spung i' your mouth,
She is so full of flegm, else sheel go near
To strangle you, and yet they say she has
A most devouring appetite to mans flesh,
You may have a devill of your own to attend you,
And when y'are melancholy,
Sheel make you Ghosts and Goblins dance before you
Bring Bears and Bandogs with an o'r grown Ape
Playing upon the gittern.

HORTENSIO
Where is this creature? shall he not see her first?

VOLTERINO
I left her in a Sive was bound for Scotland,
This morn to see some kindred, whence she was
Determin'd to take egg-shell to Skeedam.

[Enter **PANDOLPHO** disguis'd.

From thence when she has din'd she promis'd me
To ride post hither on a Distaff.

BERTOLDI
How?

VOLTERINO
Oh here she is, what think you of a Husband
Mother? can you love this Gentleman, hee's one
Will be a great comfort to you.

PANDOLPHO
I like the stripling well,
He will serve to watch my pots, and see that non
Of my spirits boil over.

BERTOLDI
Is this your Mother?
Come I'l be hang'd, tis the more hansome destiny
Unless you will take composition—

PANDOLPHO
Let me talk with the Gentleman.

HORTENSIO
I am at leisure now to wait on you sir.
Unbind, and lead him to the Duke.

VOLTERINO

Flaviano? you are the Gentleman his Highness
Gave strict command should be persu'd, I shall
Be proud to wait upon you to the Court.

FLAVIANO

I wo'not lose my passion on such bloodhounds.

BERTOLDI

We are agreed, hey, here's my pardon.

PANDOLPHO

Yes, I am satisfied, and can thank you Signior
In severall shapes—

[Discovers himself.

HORTENSIO

The Drawer!

PANDOLPHO

I did want a sum like this to set me up: I was
Provided gainst your Sword, a pretty night-cap,
And almost Pistoll proof, I shall be rich,
I thank your bounty, and so rid the Witch.

[Exit.

FLORELIA

Here's none of the Dukes hand.

VOLTERINO

It needs not Madam.
I know not yet by what device you came together thus.

HORTENSIO

I'l tell you as we walk.

BERTOLDI

Pay for a pardon and not kill my man?
The Duke shall hear o' this.

[Exeunt.

SCENE V

A Room in the Palace.

[Enter **LEONATO**.

LEONATO
No news of Flaviano yet? some furies
Have sure transported him.

[Enter **PETRONIO**.

PETRONIO
A Gentleman with Letters sir from Mantua.

[Enter **DUKE of MANTUA**.

LEONATO
Ha! admit him—leave us, the Duke himself?

DUKE
That comes to offer
A pledge for young Honorio, not in thought
Guilty of that unprincely entertainment
You had at Mantua. if my Son, as fame
Is busie in Ferrara, be expos'd
To your displeasure, change my fate with his,
That to my shame in part consented to
The practice of a Traitor Flaviano,
Who us'd my power to advance his own ambition
To your dishonour, and instead of my
Fioretta, whether now alive or dead
I know not, cheat your faith with Juliana,
To quit the noble safety your Sword brought us,
My life is troublesome in the loss of fame,
And Fioretta.

LEONATO
Where is Flaviano?

DUKE
Fled like a guilty villain from my Justice,
May hortor overtake him; let my Son
Live by some noble deeds to expiate
His Fathers forfeit, and disgrace; I come
Without a guard, and were it not a crime
To my eternity, cou'd sacrifice
My self without expecting your revenge,
Or nature to conclude my age.

[Enter **DONABELLA, FIORETTA, JULIANA.**

DONABELLA
Let me have Justice.

FIORETTA
Give me Justice Prince.

JULIANA
Let me have Justice too.

LEONATO
Against whom Sister?

DONABELLA
Against this Lady.
She hath conspir'd to take away my life.

FIORETTA
My enemy is Duke Leonato sir,
Who hath conspir'd to take away himself,
A Treasure equall with my life.

JULIANA
My enemy is Juliana sir, that hath conspir'd
To rob her self, both of her life and honour.

DUKE
Tis she, my aged eyes take leave of seeing,
Expect no object after this so welome.
My Daughter Fioretta!

FIORETTA
Dearest Father.

DONABELLA
How, Fioretta? she is then but Sister
To my Honorio, life of all my joyes,
My feet have wings at this glad news.

[Exit.

LEONATO
Were you the Suffering Lady Fioretta?
How could you live so long within the Court,
And no good Angell all this while acquaint me?

FIORETTA

This joy is too too mighty, and I sha' not
Repent my exile to be thus rewarded.

LEONATO
Confirm my happiness again, no treason
Shall now divide us.

DUKE
Your hearts grow together.

LEONATO
I have receiv'd by Claudio the particular
Of Flaviano's treason, he has guilt
Above your knowledge sir, Juliana findes it,
And is confess'd his strumpet.

DUKE
You amaze me.

FIORETTA
I bless now my suspition, when I was
Convey'd from Mantua, which directed me
To leave Placentia secretly, and invite
My self a stranger to this Court, where now
I meet as much joy as my soul can fancie.

JULIANA
You have not all this while pronounc'd my doom,
I fear you hold intelligence with my soul,
And know what pains I feel while I am living,
You will not be so mercifull to kill me.

[Enter **CLAUDIO, VOLTERINO, HORTENSIO, FLORELIA, BERTOLDI, FLAVIANO.**

CLAUDIO
Flaviano!

HORTENSIO
I present you with a Gentleman,
I took rifling a Hermit in the Wood,
As it appears in hope to scape persute,
Hid in a Friers habit, who dispatch'd
After a matrimoniall betwixt
This Lady and my self.

BERTOLDI
That old Gentleman should be Duke of Mantua
What think you sir?

CLAUDIO
And that his Daughter Fioretta.

BERTOLDI
She is my Mistris.

CLAUDIO
She is like to prove the Duchess of Ferrara.

BERTOLDI
His Grace will not use me so,
I will have Justice, Justice Gentle Duke.

FLORELIA
Are you mad?

BERTOLDI
I'l be reveng'd o' somebody.

[Enter **HONORIO** and **DONABELLA**

LEONATO
Honorio your son, to meet your blessing.

DONABELLA
This was the life I feard to lose by her,
Whom I suppos'd my rivall, pardon Madam.

DUKE
Thus circled, I must faint beneath my happiness

LEONATO
Forgive my passion, and receive a Brother.

HONORIO
That name doth honor us, where is Flaviano?

FLAVIANO
Whose witty brain must sentence me? let it
Be home and hansom, I shall else despise
And scorn your coarse inventions.

FIORETTA
Let me obtain, since providence hath wrought
This happy change, you would not stain our joyes
With any blood, let not their sins exceed our charity.

LEONATO
Let him for ever then be banish'd both
Our Duke-doms.

HONORIO
What shall become of Juliana?

DUKE
She (if your grace more fit to judge, consent)
Shall to a house of converts and strict penance,
Where Flaviano, as the price of her
Lost honor, shall pay her dowry to Religion;
What doth remain of his estate, shall be
Emploid toward the redeeming Christian Captives.

JULIANA
I chearfully obey, and call it mercy.

LEONATO
Tis a most pious Justice.

BERTOLDI
Justice, thats my kue, Justice, Justice to Bertoldi
Against Signior Volterino, I am cheated.

FLORELIA
Will you be a fool upon record?

LEONATO
You shall have Justice.
Volterino, we appoint you, till he learn
More wit, to be his Guardian, and at your
Discretion govern his estate, so leave us.

VOLTERINO
I shall with my best study manage both.

BERTOLDI
I am as good as begg'd for a fool.

LEONATO
And thus we chain our hearts and provinces.
Madam I wish you joyes, to Fioretta
I give my self, my Sister to Honorio.
Treason is sick in her short reign, but when
Heaven sees his time, Truth takes her Throne agen.

[Exeunt **OMNES**.

EPILOGUE Spoken by **JULIANA**.

Now the play's done, I will confess to you,
And wo' not doubt but you'll absolve me too.
There is a mysterie, let it not go far;
For this Confession is auricular:
I am sent among the Nuns to fast and pray,
And suffer piteous penance, ha, ha, ha,
They could no better way please my desires,
I am no Nun—but one of the Black-Friers.

FINIS.

JAMES SHIRLEY – A CONCISE BIBLIOGRAPHY

The following includes years of first publication, and of performance if known, together with dates of licensing by the Master of the Revels if available.

TRAGEDIES
The Maid's Revenge (licensed 9th February 1626; printed, 1639)
The Traitor (licensed 4th May 1631; printed, 1635)
Love's Cruelty (licensed 14th November 1631; printed, 1640)
The Politician (acted, 1639; printed, 1655)
The Cardinal (licensed 25th May 1641; printed, 1652).

TRAGI-COMEDIES
The Grateful Servant (licensed 3rd November 1629 as The Faithful Servant; printed 1630)
The Young Admiral (licensed 3rd July 1633; printed 1637)
The Coronation (licensed 6th February 1635, as Shirley's, but printed in 1640 as a work of John Fletcher)
The Duke's Mistress (licensed 18th January 1636; printed 1638)
The Gentleman of Venice (licensed 30th October 1639; printed 1655)
The Doubtful Heir (printed 1652), licensed as Rosania, or Love's Victory in 1640
The Imposture (licensed 10th November 1640; printed 1652)
The Court Secret (printed 1653).

COMEDIES
Love Tricks, or the School of Complement (licensed 10th February 1625; printed under its subtitle, 1631)
The Wedding (ca. 1626; printed 1629)
The Brothers (licensed 4th November 1626; printed 1652)
The Witty Fair One (licensed 3rd October 1628; printed 1633)
The Humorous Courtier (licensed 17th May 1631; printed 1640).
The Changes, or Love in a Maze (licensed 10th January 1632; printed 1639)
Hyde Park (licensed 20th April 1632; printed 1637)

The Ball (licensed 16th November 1632; printed 1639)
The Bird in a Cage, or The Beauties (licensed 21st January 1633; printed 1633)
The Gamester (licensed 11th November 1633; printed 1637)
The Example (licensed 24th June 1634; printed 1637)
The Opportunity (licensed 29th November 1634; printed 1640)
The Lady of Pleasure (licensed 15th October 1635; printed 1637)
The Royal Master (acted and printed 1638)
The Constant Maid, or Love Will Find Out the Way (printed 1640)
The Sisters (licensed 26th April 1642; printed 1653).
Honoria and Mammon (printed 1659)

DRAMAS

A Contention for Honor and Riches (printed 1633), morality play
The Triumph of Peace (licensed 3rd February 1634; printed 1634), masque
The Arcadia (printed 1640), pastoral tragicomedy
St. Patrick for Ireland (printed 1640), neo-miracle play
The Triumph of Beauty (ca. 1640; printed 1646), masque
The Contention of Ajax and Ulysses (printed 1659), entertainment
Cupid and Death (performed 26th March 1653; printed 1659), masque

9 7 8 1 7 8 7 3 7 3 4 7 1